Kind words from ot

"A game-changing sales and marketing system that is super easy to implement, and WOW, what a treasure trove of templates."

Amanda C. Watts, Founder of Oompf Global

- $ -

"Richard not only gives great marketing advice, but he is also fun and a joy to work with. He makes sure that I am focused and doing the right stuff to bring consistency and routine to marketing for my business.

He practises what he preaches and so has great examples to share that you can literally swipe, amend, and use immediately.

He is very practical and shows you how to do it every step of the way. This book gives the details on what each component of the sprint looks like. Great read!"

Marita Price – Founder of Hello Performance

- $ -

"Richard is a brilliant coach, and he worked with me in making my business offer an on-demand product. The Million Dollar Sprint™ is an excellent accelerator and I have benefited a lot from it."

Erefa Coker – Founder of IMO Services

- $ -

"Brilliant diversity of ideas – clearly communicated. Superb forum to generate innovative thought. I get a huge amount from these meetings – and as a result, so do my own clients."

Kevin Ahronson – Founder of The Hampshire School of Photography

"We're barely a few weeks into the program and the difference this is making and will continue to make is tangible.

We have more leads than ever before and a very clear and effective lead generation strategy that actually works (how refreshing!).

We also have more clarity than ever on the service that will allow us to scale massively in the next 12 months. The future has never looked brighter. Thank you Richard!"

Serena Sabala – Co-founder of Whole Shift Wellness

- $ -

"Great community to work with, lots of new ideas, and walk-through teaching/training for all the different areas you can work on in your business."

Danny Greeves – Founder of The Trauma Expert

- $ -

"I have been working with Richard for a year and love that he knows every aspect of lead generation.

It's been an amazing journey, and I now understand what I need to do, as, for a long time, I was unaware of what foundations I needed to put into my business.

I have thrived and scaled my business. Thank you."

Andrea A Smith – Founder of The ACE Accelerator

- $ -

"What an amazing programme to be a part of. Thoroughly enjoyed all the sessions and the value is 110%. Richard Woods is committed, knowledgeable and his expertise leads by example. If you are thinking about doing the Million Dollar Sprint™ – just do it."

Cara Cunniff – Founder of ThriveWell Global

The Million Dollar Sprint™

Zero to One Million in Revenue

How to scale a hyper-profitable service business
without investment and within 12 months

Richard Woods
Founder of the Million Dollar Sprint™

BOOK BRILLIANCE
PUBLISHING

First published in Great Britain in 2023
by Book Brilliance Publishing
265A Fir Tree Road, Epsom, Surrey, KT17 3LF
+44 (0)20 8641 5090
www.bookbrilliancepublishing.com
admin@bookbrilliancepublishing.com

A CIP catalogue record for this book is available
at the British Library.

ISBN 978-1-913770-58-7

Printed by 4edge Ltd.
Typeset in Adobe Caslon Pro.

Poppy & Mylo – it's all for you xxx

Contents

Preface 1

Introduction 5

The 8-Step Million Dollar Sprint™ System 9

Step 1: Part 1: Find your Colin and solve a pain point well and
       with a solution that scales 11

Step 1: Part 2: A scalable solution 19

Step 2: Part 1: Find and hang out with others (your audience)
       for whom you can solve this pain 25

Step 2: Part 2: How to find and hang out with your
       audience on Facebook 59

Step 3: Move them into your database 73

Step 4: Over-deliver value for free pre-sale 77

Step 5: Create a high-converting sales process that relies on
       scripts and templates – not sales talent 137

Step 6: Crank up the volume of leads through paid ads &
       automated outreach 161

Step 7: Recruit a commission-based sales team 167

Step 8: Implement a profit system to accumulate founder
       wealth alongside company growth 173

8 Steps: Conclusion 177

Next Steps 179

Acknowledgements 181

Further Reading 182

About the Author 183

Preface

It was 2015.

I was sitting in a small silver chair.

The chair was awkward, uncomfortable, and slightly lower than normal.

I guessed this was all part of the plan.

The space was vast, an entire floor at the top of a towering skyscraper from which the partitioning had been removed months ago when the last occupants left.

It now sat empty, silent, dead.

The only thing to fill it was tension.

And her.

I took a moment to take in the late-spring Sunday afternoon and the 360-degree vista of London offered by the 47th floor of the building known as 'The Cheese Grater'; a fitting name, it turned out, for what was about to happen.

It was officially just the two of us, but we were not alone.

Far from it.

"I haven't got a bloody clue what it's about."

"Crap; this is it then," I thought.

Years of work – and all those months I'd been separated from my friends, my family, my pregnant wife – for nothing.

"You've never done anything first."

I grimaced as her second remark landed, but I was on the ropes by this stage anyway. It was like kicking a dying man on the green mile, and her comments were pointless unless she was trying to make a name for herself.

She was.

This was her first outing; she needed blood and had been waiting for this opportunity.

I was easy prey – a hunter of soundbites' dream.

"Is it bullshit?"

No words came to me.

"I think it's bullshit."

I needed to turn her quickly, so I spluttered: *"I don't think it's bullshit; with this investment I'll be able to quickly scale this company…"*

"I don't believe it," she interrupted, then gave me the look that let me know it was all over.

And, just like that, my carefully worked for, hard-earned time on top BBC show *The Apprentice*, watched by 12 million people, went into freefall.

All that was left was a trip to the boardroom to meet the stubby end of Lord Sugar's finger as he told me, "You're fired!" just one week short of the final.

Third place and a bronze medal was no consolation for the amount of time and energy I'd expended.

I'd been the front-runner for 11 weeks.

I'd won 8 out of 10 tasks (second on the all-time list from 20 years of production history).

I'd broken two *Apprentice* records: one for most sales in one day (£4.3 million); one for "The best advertising task ever seen on *The Apprentice*" – credited by Lord Sugar himself.

Yet I now found myself in the back of a black cab on my way to a holding hotel to decompress.

The only respite during my three-month institutionalisation had been one 10-minute phone call per week to my wife.

"How did I throw it all away?" I asked myself as my head hit the Travelodge pillow that night.

The answer? My business plan was too complicated.

"Simplicity scales, complexity fails," kept rattling around in my head.

I promised myself to never be too complex again.

Introduction

In this book, I'll share the quickest and most viable way to scale your service business to a million in revenue and beyond.

Service sector businesses are companies who get paid for their knowledge through:

- direct training (e.g. a business coach)

- 'done with you' consultancy or training programmes

- or a 'done for you' service provider (e.g. an IT-support company or a marketing agency).

If you fall within one of the above categories and are looking to scale to and through a million in revenue, then this book is for you.

If you're looking to transition into the highly lucrative service economy but don't know where to start, again, this book is very much for you.

The truth is, the 'how' of creating a clear, repeatable system – and crazy profits from it – is easily articulated. The tough part is stopping an entrepreneurial mind from taking a bit from this book and bits from others and cobbling them together to create a Frankenstein's monster rather than the streamlined digital-enabled business you're looking for.

Distraction, hype, and complexity are your enemies – simplicity and focus are your friends.

Let the Million Dollar Sprint™ system be your friend.

Having scaled two businesses each to over a million dollars in revenue before making highly profitable exits, I've learned a thing or two about starting and growing small businesses. Today I focus on helping a select band of expert service sector entrepreneurs to do the same.

If you're reading this, congratulations! You're one of that group and are en route to a million-dollar revenue. Incidentally, thank you for inviting me along on your adventure.

When I started my business career straight after university, I wasted a few years bouncing from shiny new fad to shiny new fad, never really committing to one system long enough for it to bear fruit.

Once I realised this, however, both my business and my life took off, while my working day became less crazy, even simple.

I now spend far more time with my family, take longer breaks, and feel less stressed. I even have time for hobbies, sports, and friends – remember them?

Sounds nice – right?

But be warned: the road to a million in revenue is littered with company tombstones and entrepreneurial tears. Only the 'all in' survive, which creates one huge variable:

YOU – and your dedication.

My advice is to turn back now if you're not 100% committed.

But, if you are, then get ready, because life will get very interesting as you journey through my eight steps to the Million-Dollar Hall of Fame.

Marketing agency Yomp and heating company Boiler 24/7 –
both scaled to become Million Dollar Businesses

The 8-Step Million Dollar Sprint System™

To become a highly profitable, fast-growing service business, is as straightforward as working through my eight steps.

It's all you need to be hyper-successful, and the best part is it's super simple.

I'll start by listing the eight steps, before I focus on the key elements you need to act on and explain exactly how you create the stepping stones you'll need to make your business growth a raging success.

The book includes absolutely everything you need to scale and is designed to get you up to speed as quickly as possible. It truly is, then, your Million Dollar Bible.

Step 1

Solve a pain point well and with a solution that scales

Step 2

Find and hang out with others (your audience) for whom you can solve this pain

Step 3

Move them into your database

Step 4

Over-deliver value for free pre-sale

Step 5

Create a high-converting sales process that relies on scripts and templates – not sales talent

Step 6

Crank up the volume of leads through paid ads and automation

Step 7

Recruit a commission-based sales team

Step 8

Implement a profit system and start to accumulate founder wealth alongside company growth

Step 1
Part 1: Find your Colin and solve a pain point well and with a solution that scales

As a service provider you'll already be an expert in your field with a unique feel for your industry sector. But are you sure you haven't fallen into the 'be everything to everyone' trap?

The most successful service businesses know precisely *who* they help; the *result* they help their clients to achieve; and the *process* through which they do so.

Before starting any campaign to win new clients, first dive into your ideal client avatar to understand exactly the pain you intend to solve for them.

Go into this as deeply as you can. The more you understand, the better you'll be able to develop your solution – and the better it will solve the pain for your clients.

Ultimately, as long as you solve the right pain point, clients will spend a considerable investment to work with you.

Stay Focused

A client once described how picking a target market and a specific pain felt like having 'niche claustrophobia'. They believed their world was becoming too small and instead wanted to try to sell to two or three other potential client avatars.

I encouraged them to hold steady and to focus on building their sales and marketing systems: to go deep, not wide.

Once they'd actually deployed the templates and training we provided, and had done so consistently over several weeks, something triggered. Like lighting a touchpaper, their company started to scale so rapidly they even had to slow their marketing funnel to keep up with the speed of growth.

We never discussed moving away from their target-client niche again.

> **TIP:** Scratch your own itch. Most of the world's leading companies have been created by founders who started by solving a pain they had, and then offered it to others.

Part 1: Find your Colin and solve a pain point

I first understood the power of niche in my second business, Yomp, a marketing agency.

When I first launched, I took great pride in announcing that Yomp was a full-service digital marketing agency that worked with all types of businesses, large and small, to be the one-stop-shop that would cover all their marketing needs.

The trouble was, I got what I asked for: businesses of all shapes and sizes, all wanting different types of marketing.

One minute I'd be designing business cards for one-man bands; I even organised printing them, too. Next, I'd create an online store for a Russian faux-fur coat importer, before dashing to a meeting to discuss a Google ads campaign targeting Chinese students for a hall of residence at Southampton University.

I used to recount such stories at a local breakfast networking meeting I attended at an ungodly hour every Wednesday morning. I'd proudly report to my fellow networkers the complexity of each project, thinking they'd be impressed.

Yet after each meeting, I'd scurry round the corner to where I'd hidden my clapped-out silver Ford Mondeo Estate (lovingly named Long John Silver) and dart off before anyone could see me. Then I'd race to the office to pull another 12-14-hour day firefighting client campaigns that were all over the place.

Each day as it grew dark, the phone would finally stop ringing and my staff would go home, leaving me alone. I would reflect and know that something didn't stack up.

As a team, we made it up as we went along. Each new client represented a new skill we needed to develop as well as a new process – perhaps even specific personnel we needed to recruit.

I would start every day not knowing who to focus on first – we were being pulled in every direction from a client-delivery front. Then there was Yomp's sales and marketing, for which I was also responsible.

I had so many services and packages to promote; it was crazy. The future was not looking good, and, in a double whammy, I was about to burn out and go bust all at once.

My world looked like a set of arrows going only one inch forward but in 12 different directions. I was drained of energy.

One morning, however, I found an enquiry in my inbox from a lad in my rugby club who worked for an IT company. They were looking at their marketing, and he mentioned that Yomp might be a good fit.

We were running out of clients who hadn't lost patience with us so I immediately jumped in the car to head to a meeting with the IT company.

Once I got there, my friend wished me good luck and explained that as marketing wasn't his remit, it would be over to me to take the meeting. *"Great,"* I thought, as I looked around the plush offices, *"this looks like an epic failure in the making."* After all, why would these guys want to work with little 'have-a-go' heroes like us?

The boardroom where the meeting took place was full of sharp-suited, 'proper' grown-ups, headed by the MD, Colin, who explained that their business had big goals – and equally big expectations.

Their team of over fifty was snowballing, and they were looking for a marketing agency to generate the leads they needed to hit their targets. *"So,"* he asked, *"how would you do it?"*

Gulp …

Luckily, from the start of my career, when I launched my first website, I watched various experts talk about the new concept of content marketing and SEO. Subsequently, I was able to mix some takeaways from recent YouTube videos into my off-the-cuff presentation. I even managed to link them to client work we had recently completed for a tradeshow exhibition company.

"Content is king, Colin," I said, a little self-consciously. *"But from looking at your website, you don't have any videos or blogs, you don't produce an email newsletter, and you have only posted twice in the last month on social media. How can you hope to stand out to potential clients or climb Google's rankings if your website's nothing more than a few boring service pages?"*

"Spot on!" Colin jumped in. *"It's exactly what I've been saying to this lot."*

From that moment, he took control of the conversation – I scribbled notes faster than a shorthand reporter at a rap convention!

Roughly, Colin already knew what would work. After all, he'd been in his industry for years and had seen it all before. He just needed someone who could see what he saw, knew how to apply it, and – equally importantly – had time to do so.

"Let's keep it simple but focused," he said. *"After all: 'Simplicity scales, complexity fails.'"*

BAM! It hit me right between the eyes.

The last time I'd heard that was from Lord Sugar.

In the long term, I'd got lost following my downfall on *The Apprentice*. In the first few months after the show, my book *Digital Trailblazer* had become a bestseller. I'd appeared at numerous red-carpet events with the typical 'famous for being famous' crowd from *The Only Way Is Essex*, *Love Island*, and *Made in Chelsea*. Meanwhile, my company's phone was ringing with queries from potential clients.

Work had picked up, and from the outside, things were going well – I was rushing from client meeting to stage presentation and back again.

I was a busy fool, running around saying 'yes' to every opportunity but making no real money.

That meeting with Colin was the slap around the face I needed.

I'd promised myself never to be too complex again, yet somehow I'd filled my life with superficial noise that neither paid the bills nor created clients who needed our services.

That meeting confirmed my understanding of what 'simplicity' meant and fuelled my desire to make something extraordinary. I needed to go deeper into a solution than I'd ever dreamed possible.

It was the birthplace of Yomp's flagship lead-generation service designed for one type of client: our niche.

Essentially, Colin helped us build a service that was perfect for what his company needed.

It was 'desired result focused', i.e. he wanted leads, and the product created the focus on getting leads. It fulfilled the real pain point Colin experienced.

We were so blown away by the results that we went on to model (with his blessing) the solution we'd created into a repeatable product with common daily, weekly, and monthly tasks. As an additional bonus, it could also be optimised for both time and client results – which ultimately freed me from being stuck in delivery.

That first meeting with Colin was a Million-Dollar moment for us. We now had our 'thing' and became great at it. Our turnover – and profit – boomed.

It was my ticket out of entrepreneurial poverty and becoming a million-dollar business owner.

My world had changed. Now, it looked like this:

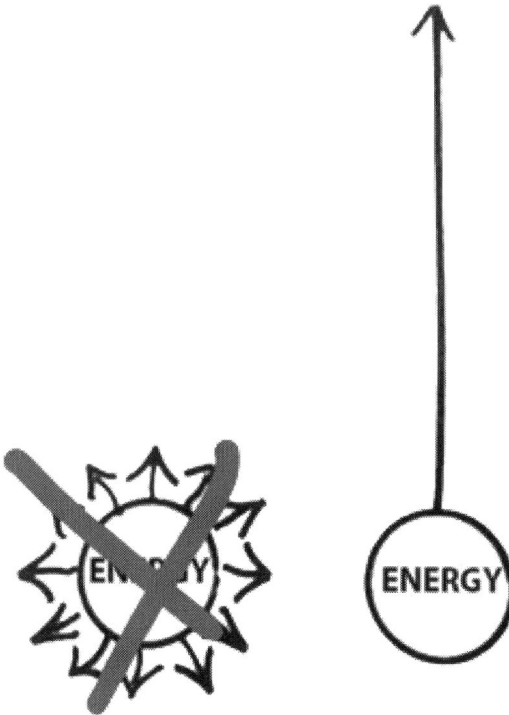

ACTION: Take a moment to visit our audience training module, then complete the worksheet to find who you're going to target and their pain point that you can solve. Scan the QR code below to download the worksheet!

Remember: you may have worked with this person before, or they may be hypothetical; they might even be the person you were before you got to where you are today. But, whoever they are, it is vital to identify them. After all, everything starts with the pain you're going to solve, and how can you solve a pain when you don't know who that someone is?

Colin Sale, the man who changed everything!

Step 1 - Part 2
A scalable solution

Now you know who to focus on and how to find a pain point to solve, how do you make it scalable?

Creating a scalable solution means understanding the hours you're willing to dedicate to your business and crafting your service around this.

I hope that your ambition is to one day remove yourself entirely from your company and for it to run like clockwork without you.

As the founder of a business, the key is not to get stuck within its delivery or sales systems. Many consultants, for example, start by focusing on one-to-one coaching as their high-ticket solution, then add a group and an online course to create a portfolio of a bronze-, silver-, and gold-style product.

In my experience, this is a recipe for disaster as you'll be trying to deliver – and make work – three tiers of client services.

Similarly, suppose you're the founder of a done-for-you service provider. In that case, the variety of solutions your company offers may grow every time you win a new client, which means you'll suddenly find yourself stuck within delivery because your service is bespoke for each client. (Not to mention the weekly project management meetings you must attend and the lengthy reports you must write.)

In both cases, selling one universal solution rather than an entire portfolio of services or programmes would be far simpler and more effective.

That way, potential clients are faced with a simple decision: Do they want to solve the pain or not?

> *Solving a client's pain does not always mean you need to be the person in your business doing the work.*

The universal solution you create is your flagship product.

When I started to look at a scalable solution for my coaching business, I realised that I was stuck under the one-to-one glass ceiling. Needing to work directly with each client meant I was incredibly stressed and overworked – yet I only had fifteen of them!

That's when I started to look at how I could work with hundreds of clients but still deliver massive value.

Enter: The Million Dollar Audience Shift™

The Million Dollar Audience Shift™ is my unique system to move your target audience within four categories:

- **Leadership:** *From* not knowing where to turn, *to* having a clear path to follow

- **Community:** *From* feeling alone with a problem, *to* finding a group of peers all striving for the same thing

- **Rhythm:** *From* not solving the problem (or sporadically trying to), *to* making the solution a habit

The Million Dollar Audience Shift
from the fringes to the centre

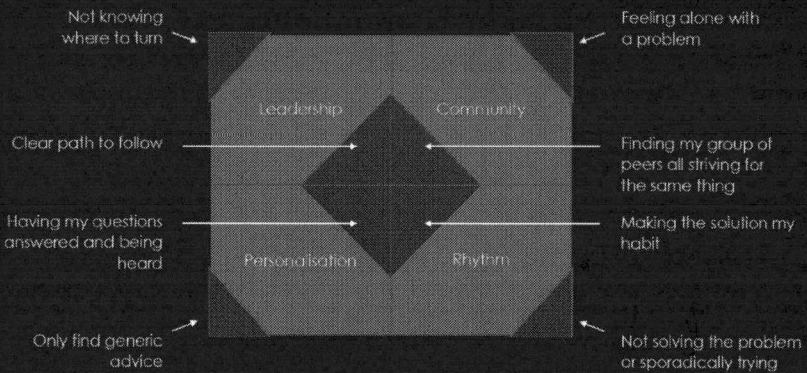

Not knowing where to turn

Feeling alone with a problem

Leadership

Community

Clear path to follow

Finding my group of peers all striving for the same thing

Having my questions answered and being heard

Making the solution my habit

Personalisation

Rhythm

Only find generic advice

Not solving the problem or sporadically trying

MDS
MILLION DOLLAR
SPRINT

From Theory to Practice

- **Personalisation:** *From* generic advice, *to* having your questions answered and your pain solved

Once you've helped your audience shift in all four categories, they'll find themselves in the sweet spot where, through working with you, they are getting great results within an immersive experience.

So, how does this work in practice for a done-for-you business and a coach/consulting business?

Consulting/Coaching: In the case of coaching, I realised that although spending time with an expert is vital, the ideas and core syllabus don't have to be delivered live – and certainly not one-to-one. Instead, they can be delivered through online learning modules, with the added benefit that these offer clients 24/7 access to the solution to their pain points.

Removing the need to deliver the core syllabus live left me free to organise regular drop-in Q&A clinics, say for one hour, three times a week, moving up to a daily session for larger volumes of clients. Here, I could offer leadership by mentoring and supporting clients at whatever stage they had reached within the programme, answering their specific questions and providing personalisation by tailoring the journey to their particular needs.

This abundance of access helped clients form a habit as they would complete a module, share their progress, and then move on to another module. The critical part was to share their progress. Weekly check-ins and tasks kept groups engaged and gave the programme rhythm, while generating a community within which clients could share their journey. Business-growth journeys can often be lonely, so introducing an aspect of community to my system was vital for me.

Once I'd moved all my one-to-one clients to the new system, efficient use of automation and delegation opportunities left me (as the expert) only needing to deliver three to four hours of flagship programme time per week, even with over 100 high-ticket clients and earning over a million in revenue as a result.

Done-For-You: The good news is that it is just as easy for done-for-you business owners to achieve a zero-hour delivery time per week.

When I started Yomp, I insisted on having my finger in every pie – in other words, I was a total control freak. As you'd expect, I quickly became the bottleneck blocking our growth, but once I realised this, I worked to create a robust process that I could hand over to a team member.

The pivotal 'a-ha' moment was realising that it wasn't so much knowing what to do each day but what the *result* needed to be. After that, we could create a journey from where the client currently was, to where they wanted to be.

Focusing on return on investment, it is easy to set – and refine – daily actions that are clear, repeatable, and delegable. I started by creating a set of checklists for each delivery element to ensure that the client achieved the desired result at each stage.

Using a project-management tool, I then created a board for each client, which contained all their checklists, making it relatively simple to project-manage the deliverables by assigning them to members of my team and/or sub-contractors.

However, I knew that clients who pay for an outsourced service expect to have catch-up meetings, receive regular reports and emails or call through any changes and/or instructions. So, how could I prevent all this from landing at my feet? The answer was to tap into the returning-to-work parent market.

All the people I chose were competent, many having held careers in the city before they'd had kids and, now their children were older, they were free to work for Yomp as part-time campaign managers. Indeed, they were perfect: not only did they have the maturity to discuss complex work at a professional level, giving clients confidence that their work would be completed on time and within budget, but they were happy to take a wage cut (receiving around £15 p/h) in return for the convenience of only working three to four hours a day, four days a week.

Most importantly, however, I no longer had to be our clients' primary point of contact, and the business had become scalable.

Step 2
Find and hang out with others (your audience) for whom you can solve this pain

Who is your audience?

To find your audience, close your eyes and picture your perfect client. How old are they? What are they wearing? What's their role within their company? How big is that company? How affluent are they? How new to their role are they? The more questions you can answer, the more precise the image of your perfect client will become.

Once you get a feel for the 'who', think about the pain you're offering to solve. After all, one creates the other – the pain is linked to the person, and the person is linked to the pain.

Remembering this simple formula might help:

$$Pa\ (pain) + Pe\ (person) = O\ (opportunity)$$

What can you help them to be faster, better, cheaper or stronger? In the end, whether you're growing a client's wealth or helping them become healthier, as a successful service-sector entrepreneur, you will apply your knowledge and help your clients overcome a specific pain.

Don't forget, a worksheet is available on our audience training to help you find who you're going to target. Scan the QR Code below.

Where is your audience?

Now you know 'who' you're selling to and 'what' you're selling, it's time to find where they hang out.

The easiest hangouts to access are social media platforms, including Facebook, LinkedIn, Instagram, TikTok and YouTube. But which should you focus on – and how?

I've been running marketing-focused businesses for over 15 years, and I've seen endless social media fads come and go. I've tried, tested, vetted, invested, and danced the funky chicken all over them – from Snapchat (does anyone even have it on their phone?) to Google+ (I went to town on this one), TikTok (no one should have to see me dancing!) and Myspace (I'm not that old – honest).

There are always self-styled gurus who jump on new platforms, gain early success, and then sell others the definitive training on how best to use them to scale their business.

The truth is, it only worked for them because they were piggybacking on the wave of interest each new platform creates – they got there first and therefore, were able to build their success quickly. As an aside, you may have noticed that while they're so glad to sell their advice, you never see them applying it to *real* marketing campaigns for *real* businesses in the *real* world.

People who buy these training courses often get overwhelmed because they don't have the early success or staying power to make it into the top tier of users who capture all the attention. Simply put, they're trying to do too many things at once.

Enter the Solution – The POWER OF ONE

Let's be honest; we all tend to overcomplicate things, so focusing on just one social platform is the fastest way to a million in revenue.

I am successful because – after trying to be all things to all people in the past – I've learnt that the winning formula is to focus on *one* thing. Only using one platform to create awareness at the top of the funnel means you only need to become excellent at that one platform which hopefully you love using anyway. That way, you'll find you drive interest from your target audience into your solution much quicker than if you were stretching yourself over several social networks.

So which should you choose? It all depends. For me, it's Facebook; for others, it's LinkedIn, YouTube, TikTok or Instagram – although it's rarely not one of these five.

I've become highly skilled on Facebook and use it to have deep conversations with people daily. I know how best to use it to gain success in my business by interacting with my target audience and sharing relevant and valuable thought-leadership with them on a daily basis.

To provide some evidence, the graph below illustrates how thanks to our one-platform focus, most of our monthly leads come from

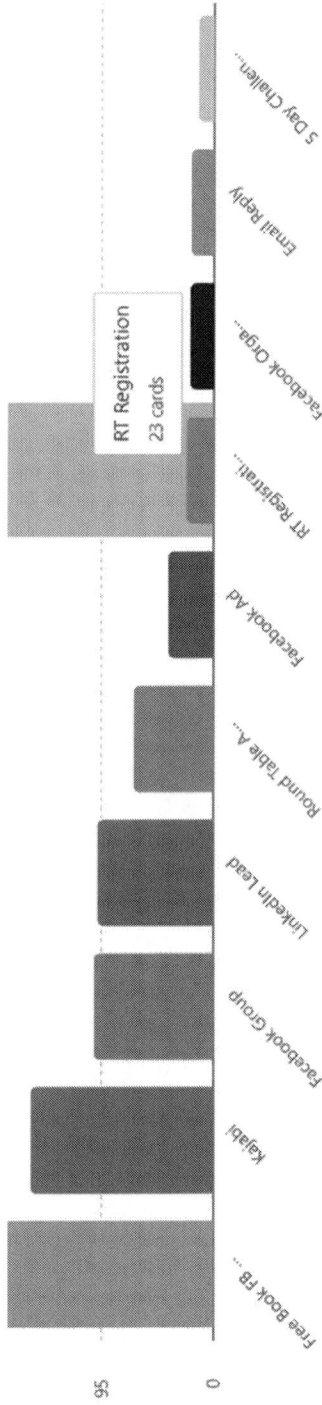

RT Registration
23 cards

5 Day Challen...
Email Reply
Facebook Orga...
RT Registrati...
Facebook Ad
Round Table A...
LinkedIn Lead
Facebook Group
Kajabi
Free Book FB...

95

0

our free book Facebook Ad and Facebook Group (positions #1 & #3), while other Facebook leads make positions #6 & #8. (N.B. 'Kajabi' is a collect-all label for unaccountable organic leads.)

We combine this with the one weekly moment when potential clients *consider* us and get to know our content before jumping into our single sales process – *convert* – where they buy just one service: The Million Dollar Sprint™.

The diagram below illustrates this with one section for *Awareness*, one for *Consider*, and one for *Convert*. The bottom section contains the three stages of your million-dollar flagship product – the one thing you *Deliver*.

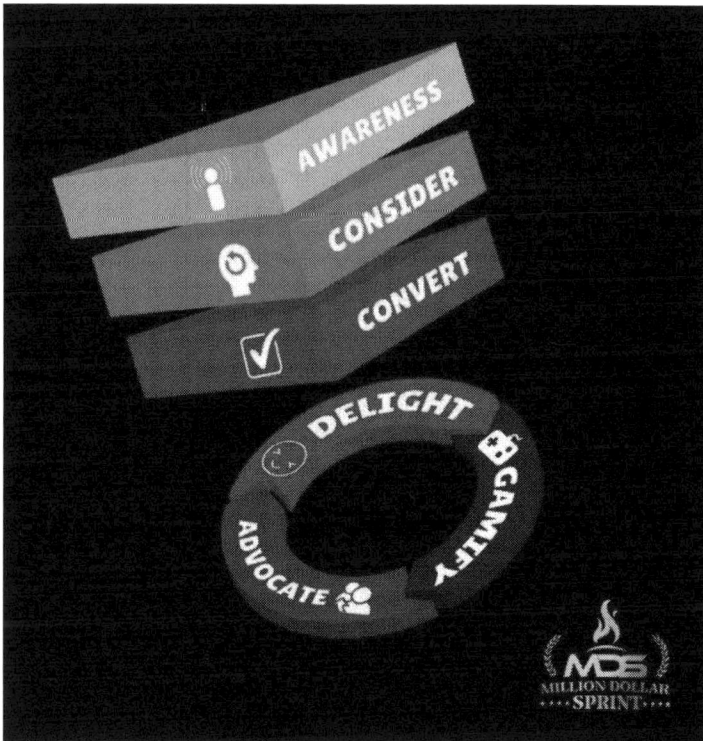

The Million Dollar Sprint™ coaching system highly recommends you choose a Facebook or a LinkedIn route, both of which can be used to facilitate awareness and consideration activity (see diagram on the following page:

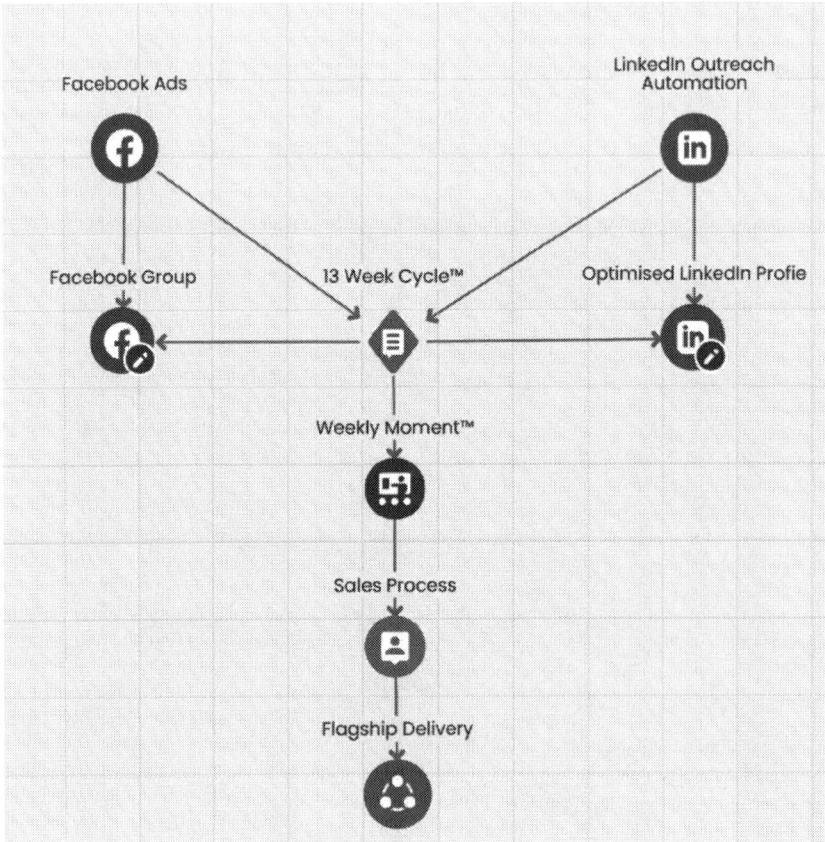

Facebook Ads

LinkedIn Outreach
Automation

Facebook Group

13 Week Cycle™

Optimised LinkedIn Profie

Weekly Moment™

Sales Process

Flagship Delivery

Going deep on one – rather than both – of these platforms is the route to success. Unless you co-own your business or have someone in your team in whom you have complete faith, you can each take responsibility for one platform each. And, if one of these two platforms doesn't stand out as more appropriate for your audience, simply ask them via a survey, research interview or by creating a simple poll on each platform and then analysing the results.

Once – by focusing on one site – you've generated maximum top-of-funnel awareness, you can relax and let the system convert prospects into clients. And rest assured, the deeper you go, the more gold you'll find. Chopping and changing or trying to do too many things at once is not the fastest way to seven figures.

Ultimately, the more you put into a platform, the more it will give back. For example, your client-acquisition targets could be relatively low if you sell a high-value service. A $3k product, say, only requires you to make around six sales a week to hit a million in revenue – and that's before you start adding in retainer fees!

> **TAKEAWAY:** Focus and go deep on one platform to build an audience and community and you will quickly achieve a small volume of sales each week. In time, you can scale – using Facebook Ads or automation such as LinkedIn outreach software Expandi – and you'll soon be rocking and rolling!

How to find your audience

Now you've chosen your platform, the next step is to find and hang out with your audience there – so let's start with LinkedIn.

LinkedIn Lead-Generation

LinkedIn can be an excellent hunting ground for new clients. It is a pure business community where users expect to discuss opportunities and make connections.

From a lead-generation perspective, the first step is to optimise your profile. The second is to set up an outreach direct message campaign to target the best options for your business via a series of messages over several weeks.

Once you have a system to cultivate appointments, you must continue expanding your network and growing your connections. And, when done correctly, Million Dollar Sprinters can expect their outbound LinkedIn efforts to generate:

- **2-3 strategy sessions per week**

- **5-6 Weekly Moment™ bookings per week on top of your thirteen-week cycle**

- **50-60 new connections per week**

- **A considerable amount of new traffic visits your profile each week**

- **Substantially increased LinkedIn social-selling index**

Fortunately, LinkedIn outbound marketing boils down to comforting simplicity for those unsure where to start: **hit the *right* people with the *right* message at the *right* time.**

This concept is *precisely* where any successful campaign starts.

For whom does LinkedIn outreach work?

When I present the power of LinkedIn to new Sprinters who sell direct to consumers, such as PTs, nutritionists and domestic service providers (not business to business), many think it's not for them. And I understand their reluctance because LinkedIn is positioned as a business network, so they probably wouldn't think of going there first for non-business information and suppliers.

Yet like all networks, LinkedIn is human-to-human first, regardless of whether you sell to consumers or businesses. And the results we've achieved for direct-to-consumer service providers have been just as fantastic as those we've earned for B2B service providers such as coaches, marketing agencies, SaaS products and recruiters.

I had excellent personal success from a B2C perspective on LinkedIn, selling hundreds of boiler services to domestic households. And what I learnt can be summed up in three words: Specialise, specialise, specialise.

Once you've got that right, everything else will follow.

For LinkedIn, lead–generation positioning is everything

How you present yourself to your target audience is often the significant difference between a successful outreach campaign and one that fails.

The Million Dollar Sprinters smashing it on LinkedIn have a well-defined value proposition and a clear idea of their target market.

Precise targeting consists of knowing the pain you solve for clients and the ultimate result they want to achieve from working with you. But getting your positioning 100% perfect can be difficult. It is based on industry experience, matching your clients' priorities, being concise and solving a problem.

If you are testing new markets, channels, or value propositions, then taking the time to get your positioning right might not always be a viable option.

If that's the case, here is a quick formula that will get you 80% of the way: **I help X do Y through Z**, where X is your target customer, Y is the benefit or value you bring them and Z is how you do it.

For example, in the case of Million Dollar Sprint™: **We help service-sector entrepreneurs scale to a million in revenue through our award-winning business accelerator.**

Optimise your LinkedIn profile

Of course, now you have a formula for presenting yourself, it is time to make sure your prospects see it.

For Sprinters who have never optimised their profiles for lead generation, this may feel slightly alien as we're going to stop talking about *you*.

Instead, it's all about your prospects.

The people you are reaching out to have their own goals and priorities, so it's your job to show you understand that and that you are the best person to get them to where they want to be.

To achieve this, I advise you to take six immediate steps, plus a seventh that you can work on over time:

1. A **headline** targeted at your specific audience

2. A **photo and banner** focused on your particular audience

3. An **'about'** section written like a sales letter

4. A targeted **'work experience'** section

5. **Endorsement** to increase your credibility

6. Good-quality posts **pinned to increase trust**

7. **Un-connect**.

1. Headline targeted at your specific audience

Your headline (1-3 lines under your name) is the first thing prospects will read after seeing your profile picture, so you need to ensure a memorable first impression. It is often described as the most important real estate on LinkedIn, especially as it shows up in more places than you might think, including:

- When someone sees a message from you in their LinkedIn inbox

- When you create a new post, and it shows up in a prospect's news feed

- In the 'people, you may know' suggestions

- At the very top of your profile page

- In the 'people who have viewed your profile' section

- In your connections list.

In short, where you go, it goes – so it is vital to get it right.

A good starting point is to avoid falling into the trap of most headlines you see on LinkedIn. 'CEO at' or 'Founder of' [Company Name] might be exemplary if you use your profile as a personal recruitment tool. However, to maximise your lead-generation potential, you need to make your headline work hard. Remember, you rely on it to reach out to your audience, make new connections, and call them to action.

Here are a few quick pointers:

- You only have 120 characters (including spaces) – so make them count

- Don't just describe who you are and what you do; include a benefit to viewers as well

- Use commas or vertical bars (|) to separate phrases

- Avoid symbols such as ◊ or ➡. They might make your headline pop, but not necessarily in a good way

- Never use all uppercase letters.

The highest-quality headlines come in two parts.

Part 1 is about **who** and **how** you help. It is the first thing new prospects will read, so it needs to speak directly to them.

Remember: the riches are in the niches, so double down on your perfect target audience and say **who** you help. (My headline, for example, starts with: "I help service-sector entrepreneurs ...")

For **how**, focus on the results you create for clients and the pain they had before. (So, the first part of my headline reads: "I help service-sector entrepreneurs sprint to a million in revenue.")

Now it's your turn:

Who you help: _____

How you help: _____

Part 2 is **why** prospects should listen, and this is where you need to squeeze in as much credibility as possible. The critical point is that this credibility must be relevant to your audience, or there's no point in adding it. And make it easy to read by separating it from part 1 with a vertical bar.

Therefore, my headline reads: "I help service-sector entrepreneurs sprint to a million in revenue | Award-Winning Entrepreneur, Author & BBC *The Apprentice* Finalist."

Now it's your turn:

Why they should listen: _____

An excellent example is offered by the image of Million Dollar Sprinter Jeremy Cooper's LinkedIn profile below:

Now form your headline by adding your three lines together to create a complete statement:

Your headline: _____

_____

_____

> **TAKEAWAY:** Remember, your headline is all over LinkedIn and is your chance to hook a prospect's attention, ultimately leading them to visit your profile and take further action.

2. Photo and banner focused on your specific audience

According to LinkedIn data: "LinkedIn profiles with professional head shots receive roughly 14 times more profile views and are 36 times more likely to receive a message on LinkedIn."

It is essential to look professional, hard-working and approachable as your photo is your shop window. But what does 'professional' look like in your case?

As a guide, I would suggest doing some brief research so you can base your profile picture on the photos your prospects use. If, for example, your target audience is the software developer community, but your photo shows you suited and booted, looking super formal, you may find they're put off. And yes, people make assumptions about you based on your photo within seconds. On the other hand, if your plan is to target financial services, the same image is probably perfect.

After all, 'people buy people', so if your audience can relate to you, you're on to a winner from the start.

TIP: The free tool PFPMaker [https://pfpmaker. com] is fantastic – it allows you to replace the original background from your photo or image with a professional (or even a crazy!) one.

Your LinkedIn banner is also one of the first things people see when they visit your profile. Located above the introduction area, it can impact a prospect's perception of you and your business within seconds.

That is why making the extra effort to create a customised, professional and eye-catching banner that makes you stand out, is so important.

Use it to reinforce your headline by showing **who** and **how** you help and **why** people should listen. The best banners do this without repeating the words from their headline; many use images.

TIP: From a design perspective, Canva has some excellent templates you can use as a starting point: https://www.canva.com/linkedin-banners/ templates/)

Remember: Your target audience must find your banner and profile photo appealing. So, once you have the digital images ready, why not ask your audience what they think by setting up a poll with a few examples? Not only will it drive interaction and feedback, but it will also build awareness. You can also share them in the Million Dollar Sprint™ community– you'll find we're always delighted to provide feedback!

3. 'About' section written like a sales letter

LinkedIn's 'about' section – the block of information that sits near the top of your profile – is an opportunity to drive sales and engage with your audience from the very beginning. As such, it should be approached as if you were writing a sales letter to your dream client.

LinkedIn doesn't make you fill this in (unlike other sections) , but here are some reasons why you should:

- **To generate attention:** Highlight facts and figures – such as key metrics about your performance or details on your clients' successes – to keep prospects interested in you.

- **To promote your USPs:** Outline what makes you stand out from the crowd and your competitors.

- **To drive action and generate leads:** Add a strong call to action such as 'join my group' or 'come to my weekly moment' followed by a link or details of how to join.

- **It is a crucial part of your public-facing profile:** If you Google your name, your LinkedIn profile is generally one of the first results. It also means your 'about' section is the first information prospects read about you.

Now I've convinced you it is worth taking time to craft a strong 'About' section, what is the best way to achieve this?

We have all come across someone who used it to write an entire novel, and chances are that you skipped over it. (I know I did!) But what makes a perfect 'About' summary?

Your LinkedIn 'About' summary should:

- be clear and concise

- demonstrate value

- be all about your target prospects

- set you up as the solution to their pains

- provide a strong call to action.

To help you, I have identified five clear sections that must be included.

As you work through each section, remember that features are a vehicle to carry value, *not* the value itself. And if you find it challenging to distinguish values from features, this might help:

- **Features:** "We built X, Y, Z."

- **Value:** "We help you make more money/save time/find freedom through X, Y, Z."

I think you'll agree which of these statements has the most impact.

The more specific you are, the more successful your summary will be and when you include metrics to support your claims, it will be even better!

It will probably take a few edits to perfect, but the following tried and tested framework will ensure that you cover each of the key and critical elements.

1. **Am I for you?**
   The first section lets readers know who you work with and what you do for them. You need to ensure that you impress them with the results of your service as ultimately that is what they are interested in achieving.

2. **How I do it**

   A short overview of your process or system – just a quick bird's eye view, one that's not too deep in detail.

3. **What my clients think**

   This evidence is where you back up your claims using one or two well-selected testimonials.

4. **My journey**

   Provide a synopsis of how you got to where you are today. Make sure it backs up what you do – the idea is to create trust with your readers.

5. **Call to action**

   The all-important next steps. Now that readers know more about you ('awareness'), it is time to move them into spending time with you and consuming some value ('consideration'). To achieve this, invite them to join your weekly moment, subscribe to your podcast, or download an info swap – whatever you have that gives value to prospects.

To illustrate the above system in action, here is a copy of my current 'about' section:

AM I FOR YOU? Through systematic lead generation, I help ambitious service-sector entrepreneurs scale to a million in revenue.

Ultimately, you get to focus on working with your clients rather than worrying about where the next one is coming from.

HOW I DO IT: I work with you to create an online event series rolled out over thirteen weeks and repeated four times a year, thus delivering an evergreen content strategy that drives attendees and raises your profile.

The attendees get wowed by your weekly presentation, then book into sales calls as warm leads for you to convert.

WHAT MY CLIENTS THINK: *I'm proud to have found Richard Woods and his amazing program, The Million Dollar Sprint™. Richard has such a professional, dedicated, laser-focused and result-driven program that he takes great pride in delivering to help his clients create their ultimate success. I am truly grateful to have had his help in the areas where I lacked knowledge and skills, which he helped me piece together. I am pleased to say it has helped me fly again with great success. He truly delivers what he says. He is honest, sincere and a true professional.*

Ghazala Jabeen – No.1 Marketing Machine

MY JOURNEY: *After scaling two businesses to a million in revenue and achieving lucrative exits from both, I now dedicate my life to helping others do the same.*

My passion for helping service-sector entrepreneurs has been prominent throughout my career, having published two bestselling business books (Digital Trailblazer and Brexitpreneurship).

My flair and passion for sales and marketing were highlighted during my appearance on BBC's 'The Apprentice' in 2015 – where I finished 3rd. I was the top seller across all tasks, and won 8 out of 10 tasks (second on the all-time list) and broke two Apprentice records: one for most sales in one day (£4.3 million) and one for "The best advertising task ever seen on The Apprentice" – credited by Lord Sugar.

My business achievements have gained further recognition through winning several national awards, such as Young Entrepreneur of the Year (Haines Watts), Key Person of Influence Award (Dent Global), and Marketing Campaign of the Year (Inspire Business Awards).

CONNECT WITH ME: *There are two ways I want to continue to help:*

#1. I host a complimentary weekly event named 'The Marketing Round Table' for service-sector entrepreneurs and would love you to come as my guest. Each week we share new ideas and methods for flooding your funnel with prospects: https://www.milliondollarsprint.com/ WeeklyMarketingRoundTable

#2. I propose you attend a Million Dollar Sprint Strategy Session, described by one attendee as "The most valuable 90 minutes I have spent all year" https://www.milliondollarsprint.com/MDS-Strategy-Session-Application

Now it's your turn:

AM I FOR YOU? _____

_____

HOW I DO IT: _____

_____

WHAT MY CLIENTS THINK: _____

_____

MY JOURNEY: _____

_____

CONNECT WITH ME: _____

_____

4. Targeted 'work experience' section

It is essential to take the time to update your work experience, knowing that your dream client is about to read it.

Are you delighted with how it flows?

Is it even up to date?

Most of all, does it add credibility to your positioning in the mind of your target audience?

We have all experienced crappy first steps on the employment ladder, but are they relevant here?

Less is always more, so purge the irrelevant, then treat what's left like an achievement-highlights reel.

For extra brownie points and to capture attention, add specific numbers and results: "I increased sales by $1.4 million", "We sold the business for eight figures", "I received the highest ratings (92%) for leadership in xyz ..."

5. Endorsement to increase your credibility

Endorsements have two prominent roles in the optimisation of your profile. First, they act as micro-testimonials in which your audience gives a collective thumbs-up to your specific expertise. Second, they highlight which skills you are an expert in – so make sure you add skills to your profile that you want people to endorse.

Your Credentials rise with the volume of endorsements you receive for each skill; essentially, they're a credibility crowd-sourcing activity. The higher your credibility, the more likely your content will go viral – particularly if you mirror the keywords from your endorsed skills with the hashtags you use on posts.

And remember, the more you give, the more you get. Not only are connections notified when you endorse them, making them more likely to return the favour, but in my experience, they'll also become more receptive to your direct message campaigns.

6. Good-quality posts pinned to increase trust

Currently, you can pin five posts to your LinkedIn profile, which means you get to highlight the most critical points you want your audience to see.

However, these five posts aren't equal, as only the first three are visible from a desktop (prospects will need to scroll across for the final two), so it makes sense for these three to be your primary focus.

Think about what you would like your dream client to see. I recommend a mix of credibility assets, thought-leadership posts and testimonials/wins, blended with a strong call to action.

Regarding the call to action, go for the next step in the funnel. Once a prospect has become 'aware' of you (by visiting your profile), your goal is to move them to a 'consideration' asset (such as your Weekly Moment™), so make this your call to action.

7. Un-connect

Let's be honest; we all started on LinkedIn by connecting with friends and colleagues. The 'randoms' began to reach out, and because we were new, we accepted a few, and before we knew it, we had hundreds, if not thousands, of weird and wonderful connections clogging up our feed.

Some of the information we see is interesting, but much is a distraction.

We've all been through this cycle, so how do we break it?

I think the best way is by locking in your target audience. Then slowly remove anyone who doesn't match your dream client.

Does a world where you have 3-4,000 connections, all perfect for your flagship product, sound like a fantasy?

I assure you it's easy.

Review your connections and delete the ones who aren't your target audience. If you have thousands, you don't need to do it all at once.

Once you've done, you can focus on producing high-quality content for your dream client avatar and sharing information they will love.

That way, they will engage with your content. The higher the engagement, the higher the number of your connections who'll see your posts. And – because your contacts are similar and your content is designed with them in mind – they'll also 'like' it, increasing the potential of your content to go viral.

More interaction with your dream client equals more leads and sales – simple!

So, now that you are confident about presenting yourself to prospects, let's start your outreach to engage with them.

Start engaging

The critical objective of outreach activity is to fill the top of your funnel and build awareness en-masse.

Sprinters see the most success when considering LinkedIn as a conversation starter. In other words, it is generally not the right place to ask for something big.

Nor is it the place to tell someone every feature your service provides or every detail of your life story.

But it is an excellent place to start things in a way that can lead to more detailed conversations further down the road.

Once a prospect has raised their hand, crucially, it is important to know where you want to take them.

Earlier, we discussed having a 'consider' asset to which you move prospects from 'awareness', which should, I hope, make the next step obvious. A good example might be: *"Come to my round table"*, or *"Subscribe to my podcast"*.

Your aim is to create an outreach campaign targeting your business's best opportunities via automated connection requests and follow-up messages.

You may need several refinements to nail your messages, so I suggest you send them manually and then fine-tune them depending on the response. Your goal is to create a near-perfect set of templates which can be sent by using automate software tools.

Finding your target audience

Engagement starts with reaching out to the right people.

Now that your profile is clearly tailored to attract your ideal audience, it's time to find them.

The most obvious place to start is the LinkedIn search bar and the wonderful world of Boolean searches.

If you haven't come across them before, Boolean search strings allow you to perform complex and targeted searches that will help to increase your focus and give far more accurate results.

They're available in the free version of LinkedIn, although they tend to be more reliable in Sales Navigator, LinkedIn's sales insights tool.

I will go into some detail here but lean into it. Nobody said growing a million-dollar business would be easy, and this is one of the elements that will help you level up your ability and your business.

LinkedIn Boolean Search

A LinkedIn Boolean search uses a set of different statements to combine, group, or exclude keywords.

Use it within the keyword field (as well as the company and title fields for Sales Navigator users). These statements are as follows:

- Quotes ["']
- AND
- OR
- NOT
- Parentheses [()]

Quotes ["'] – Quotation Marks

Putting your search term in quotation marks tells LinkedIn to match your query exactly, which makes the results far more accurate. If you search for "Managing Director" without quotation marks, for example, the results will not only include people with this in their job title and/or elsewhere in their profile, but people who are a "Director" of a "Managing" company.

To tell LinkedIn that the words in your search must appear next to each other, put your search term in quotation marks: "Managing Director".

If you don't, although at first, you may think it's great to have such a substantial list of potential prospects, once you start sifting through, you'll find many of them don't align with your ideal customer. This is why quotation marks – by filtering out those which are irrelevant – are a vital first step in refining your results.

AND

The second step is the link phrase: 'AND'. (But remember it must be in capitals, the lowercase doesn't work.)

Use 'AND' when you want to include more than one part in your search. For example, to look for IT Managers who work in the financial services sector, by using AND creating the string "IT Manager" AND "financial services", you'll bring up results for people in that specific role (IT Manager) in that particular industry (financial services).

The more ANDs you include, the more your results are targeted. (Although if you try to get too targeted, you may eventually find no results are returned.)

OR

These days, variety is the spice of life – not least regarding job titles or industry descriptions!

So this is where 'OR', which allows you to group different searches, comes into its own.

To search for people working in a particular function and at a certain level, for example, ensure you cover all bases by including as many of their potential job titles as possible.

If you're searching for marketing directors, say, you could expand your search by including similar titles for the same job: "Marketing

Director", OR "Head of Marketing", OR "VP of Marketing" OR "CMO" OR "Chief Marketing Officer".

Doing the same for the industry sector or location will enrich the accuracy of your searches.

NOT

So now you know how to add different titles, what if you want to exclude roles, locations, sectors – or even individual companies?

By excluding people/results, you don't need, using 'NOT' will make results more manageable. Consequently, helping you create a clean and easy-to-use list of potential prospects.

For example, you might use "Managing Director" NOT "Retail" to find only Managing Directors who don't run retail firms.

Parentheses [()]

By this point, you have probably realised that searches can be long and parentheses can order the importance of multiple statements within each search.

Simple strings – "Managing Director" AND "IT", for example – don't require parentheses. However, suppose you want to widen this to search for multiple job roles within a specific industry or industries – ("Managing Director" OR " CEO") AND ("IT" OR "Technology Services"), for example. In that case, the parentheses tell LinkedIn that the job titles are one part and the industry sectors another.

It keeps things tidy and makes it easy for algorithms to understand.

Final thoughts

Boolean searches may seem intimidating at first, but in a few weeks, you'll have fine-tuned your search strings enough to begin the process of finding your target audience.

The next step, then, is to start hanging out with them.

Starting Conversations

Now the foundations for your outreach are in place – you know who you want to reach out to and how you want to position yourself – it is time to start sending relevant and valuable messages.

In essence, outreach has two simple steps:

1. Send connection requests

2. Drip-feed messages over time.

So now, let's break each of these down.

Step 1: Send Connection Requests

There are three significant points to keep in mind when sending connection requests:

1. Initially, sending connection requests to people you might not know can feel a bit weird, but as that is precisely the purpose of LinkedIn, send away.

2. Currently, you can send a maximum of 100 requests per week (although Sales Navigator allows you to move that closer to 60–100 per day).

3. If you decide to use Sales Navigator, ramp your volume up slowly. Otherwise, going from sending a connection request every few days to 50 in a day might trigger LinkedIn's

security measures! Start with five the first day, ten the next, then 20, etc., until you hit 60+.

When it comes to the connection process itself, you want it to be natural and to give the reason you've reached out which can be as simple as mentioning a common industry, job title, or a company change.

You also want the request to be conversational, but remember: there's a 300-character limit, so make it short, sweet, and a solid foundation to build upon. As an example, here's one I have used:

> **Message 1:** *Hi [insert first name], it's Richard – just a friendly Coach-to-Coach hello; how's this crazy upside-down world for you?*

Notice how my message contains a zero-sales pitch. I'm starting a conversation and reassuring the connections I'm not a thread or a spammer.

Step 2: Drip-Feed Messages Over Time

Once someone's accepted your connection request and replied to your connection message, you can move the conversation towards your Weekly Moment™ – or even straight to a strategy session if the chat is going super well.

However, if they've accepted your connection request but not replied to your connection message, then start drip-feeding messages by following up with a second a couple of days after you've connected.

Once again, remember you're not trying to sell; spark a conversation.

An example might be:

Message 2: *"Awesome to connect [insert first name]; I'm one of those guys who says 'hi' to my network (a novel concept on LinkedIn these days!). So, what's the big thing you're working on right now?"*

If you haven't heard back four days after sending this second message, it is time to add a bit of credibility and a subtle call to action.

Don't, however, ask them to do anything; include a suggestion they should check something out:

Message 3: *"Crazy few days last week [insert the first name], we had over 30 coaches join our free weekly Marketing Round Table (www.milliondollarsprint.com/ WeeklyMarketingRoundTable). How was your week?"*

Note how as I'm targeting coaches in this example, I'm careful to use the word 'coaches' in my message to spike interest and highlight its relevance to them.

I also mentioned that over 30 coaches attended to provide social proof that the event was popular. I made a point of saying it's a free weekly event. Hence, prospects understand how easily they can join in.

But most of all, notice how I did it all in a short sentence that wasn't too 'salesy'.

If they still haven't replied four days or so later, think of your fourth message as a nudge. It offers you a final, short shot at getting them to act and should be your most direct call to action yet:

Message 4: *"Just bubbling this up to the top of your inbox – would you like to come next Wednesday to the above event? I'm sure you'll enjoy it and take away a ton of value."*

You can experiment with more messages, but we've settled on a four-part sequence to deliver value without the risk that constant messaging can have on a brand.

As always, keep it short, sweet, and straightforward.

Converting your audience to the next stage of the funnel

Now connection requests and follow-up messages are going out, and responses are starting to pile up in your inbox, it's time to move connections further along your sales process.

Remember, though, you're still finding and hanging out with your audience, i.e. they're still at the top of the funnel at the 'awareness' stage.

1. **Start conversations**

   While most cold outreach pushes directly for a sale, initiating a conversation with prospects on LinkedIn is about starting a relationship to get your foot in the door.

   You aren't making a hard pitch in most of your messages, so you won't always get a stern business response.

   Instead, people may ask about your business: what you do, who you serve, and how you can help them.

   Or they may strike up a seemingly random conversation about mutual interests.

   If you are new to this type of outreach, you might find this problematic initially, but in reality, these conversations are where all the benefits lie.

   You start by simply chatting with someone; once you've built up some trust, you can move things on to a sales conversation.

So don't dive into this form of outreach thinking you need to sell, sell, sell. Instead, start with a conversation.

2. Don't try to sell your flagship product; focus on selling the next stage in the funnel

The biggest mistake you can make when someone asks you to tell them more about what you do is to respond with a breakdown of everything you do and why they should buy it.

You will get no takers.

Remember, people like to buy and don't like you to sell to them.

Your goal is to create sufficient interest to move the conversation with them from LinkedIn to attending your Weekly Moment™, a virtual coffee or even – although only if they're qualified and the conversation has gone very well – straight to a strategy session.

Never try to close the deal on LinkedIn. Instead, let the conversation naturally transition to the next stage of the funnel, where you can make the actual sale.

3. Research prospects before responding

When you have several unread messages, it is tempting to fire off answers and finish interacting with them quickly.

For the best results, though, take a few minutes to research each prospect and craft a personal response according to what you learn. You could compliment them about a recent post or something they've shared, for example.

It shows you're interested and attentive.

4. Ask Questions

One of the fastest ways to kill a conversation on LinkedIn is to give a pitch and wait for a response.

Instead, ask questions to keep the conversation moving. That way, once it is focused on the values you can provide, you can request to transition to a phone call or appointment.

Questions are the foundation of a good conversation, and good discussions build trust.

So always remember to ask questions and to talk about your prospect more than you talk about yourself.

LinkedIn: Final Thoughts

Remember your purpose is to locate your dream client, connect with them and then build a conversation. It would be best if you approached LinkedIn with this mindset (which is why I named this stage 'find and hang out').

At this stage, concentrate on building potential. You can move the conversation off LinkedIn to somewhere where you have more control of the narrative later.

So be friendly, have some fun, be a bit left field and ask a load of questions!

Step 2 - Part 2
How to find and
hang out with your
audience on Facebook

After the technicalities of using Boolean searches on LinkedIn, if Facebook is your platform of choice… Congratulations, you get a far simpler ride!

In 2018, Facebook announced its mission to become community-focused. By tailoring the platform towards groups and creating millions of micro-communities, its strategy was to encourage people of similar interests to meet, network, collaborate and share.

The beauty of this approach for marketeers reflects the idiom, "birds of a feather flock together," which means your target market is probably hanging out together in one group.

All you need to do then is find that group.

The good news is that it is surprisingly easy. Head to the 'Groups' area and use the search bar at the top of the page.

However, start by thinking hard — and in different directions — about your perfect client and the types of groups in which they might be a member.

Commonly, groups take one of the following forms:

- **Industry- or role-specific**

  Most professional groups or trades have governing bodies to help them keep up to date with industry-specific news or qualifications.

  If so, then the likelihood is that there will also be a Facebook group to foster these conversations and offer support, so all you need to do is find it and apply to join.

  It may feel a little odd at first, but once (by scrolling through the history) you see the questions being asked, you'll quickly spot how to start a conversation by offering help and adding value.

- **Influencer-based**

  The rise of the influencer has been fast, and I am sure there are many people your audience already follows. The good news is they also tend to have Facebook groups.

  As a rule of thumb, the more high-profile the influencer, the larger the group – and the easier it will be for you to add value. Make sure the influencer is relevant to your audience.

  Tony Robbins, Guy Kawasaki and Karren Brady are all influencers with an audience that business owners might like to hang out with.

- **Software-based**

  Many industries use specific software, the providers of which have their user groups. And, if you find the right one, they can be a gold mine.

  I know my clients use email-marketing software, so I'm a member of the ActiveCampaign and Mailchimp groups. I have also found success in the Kajabi user group – remember, you don't necessarily need to be an expert to add value.

- **Solution-based**

  But what if the people you're targeting don't fit into a simple demographic? People who are overweight, say, or want to grow their wealth?

  In cases like these, a solution-based group is a great place to start. People looking to lose weight might try a particular diet, while those looking to grow their wealth might join a Real Estate Investments group or a cryptocurrency one. Even if you disagree with the solution the group focuses on, the people in it are looking for help, and you could be their next step.

- **Podcast-based**

  Popular podcasts often have Facebook groups where listeners and fans can interact and ask questions. Groups associated with podcasts that your dream clients are likely to listen to, can be a great place to find and hang out with your audience. The Million Dollar Sprint™'s audience, for example, tends to follow 'The Diary Of A CEO with Steven Bartlett' or 'The Tim Ferriss Show'.

Group selection criteria

When thinking about which groups to join, never join one just because you suspect your audience may be in there.

The key is to go deep, not wide. I would recommend you select only five, which gives you one group for each day of the week. I will be returning to why a daily group is useful later, but for now: Trust me -- and make your choice count!

The following criteria will help you to choose wisely:

1. **High engagement:** Ensure the group has daily posts to avoid prospecting in a ghost town. You can quickly check its activity level under the group's name in search results.

2. **People looking for help:** Only join communities that are 'open to being open'. To check this, scan the group's history to see if members ask questions and offer help.

3. **Networking-friendly:** Avoid dormant groups. A strong community will have people chatting and commenting back and forth on posts. If they're not, it is a sign the group is stale, and you're probably better elsewhere.

4. **Target audience:** It is always worth double-checking this by looking at a selection of profiles.

5. **Can you add value?:** Even if your audience is there, if they're all talking about a highly technical or left-field topic, you may be unable to add value as frequently as you would like. If so, it's time to move on.

> **TIP:** To focus your activity, regularly audit the groups you are in. (After all, most of us tend to collect groups over time.) Exiting non-relevant groups is the best way to guarantee your feed only contains posts by your target audience – leaving you free to become hyper-focused on lead generation.

Now it's your turn:

Make a list of your five target groups now:

Group 1: _____

_____

Group 2: _____

_____

Group 3: _____

_____

Group 4: _____

_____

Group 5: _____

_____

Hanging out with your audience on Facebook

Start by priming your profile so that it targets your dream client, just as previously discussed in the case of LinkedIn. However, unlike LinkedIn, Facebook doesn't position itself as primarily business-facing, so it's OK to reveal more of your personality.

Remember: People buy people, so be yourself.

And don't fret about personal posts going to relative strangers – if those you are targeting are the type of client who is more likely to be on Facebook than LinkedIn, rest assured they'll also be sharing their lives.

Another reason to focus on your profile (rather than your page) is its much higher reach. Also, as many Facebook groups don't let pages join, you will need to join under your profile. Pages can only 'follow', rather than 'friend', someone – meaning prospects have to work much harder to notice your posts.

For those who've never thought about prospecting correctly on the platform, don't worry that your friends will think you've gone all 'business-y' on them. Because Facebook offers the option of categorising people, you can easily create one category for friends and another for prospects. Then all you have to do is choose to make a post public (i.e. open to all) or limit it to just one category.

That way, you can only share pictures of your kid's football match with friends while only sharing invites to your Weekly Moment™ with prospects. It is precisely this public/private, friends/business approach that has helped many Sprinters use their Facebook profile for marketing with such fantastic success.

Next, you need to tweak three specific areas of your profile to ensure it includes the key features to move your audience to the next stage of your funnel.

1. Header

This feature is an image that should communicate both your value and why your audience should listen to you. A professional header with a call to action, such as:

"Join my Marketing Round Table for Service-Sector Entrepreneurs next Wednesday at 9 am UK time."

demonstrates what you're all about, who you work with, and the next step prospects should take.

2. Headline

This feature is the short sentence that sits below the header. As it allows fewer characters than on LinkedIn, you won't be able to pull off the same trick who and how you help and why people should listen. Still, you can at least include a clickable link (make sure to add 'https://' before it), which offers a substantial benefit as you can link away from Facebook directly to the next step in your funnel – to your Weekly Moment™, for example. Or, if the next step is your 'open to all' group on Facebook, link to that.

Because of this ability to link, I would strongly suggest you choose a pure call to action for your headline. For example:

"I run a free, weekly event for service-sector entrepreneurs called

The Marketing Round Table:

https://www.milliondollarsprint.com/marketingroundtable"

People you mix within your target Facebook groups will check out your profile and see your header and call-to-action link right underneath it.

With the right wind in their sails, prospects will click and move straight to 'consider'.

3. Link and 'about'

The final part of your profile is the 'about' info, where you can include another link. Aim to make this link focus on your 'consideration' activity, too. You may have a free group to promote your Weekly Moment™, for example, to have your headline promoting one and the link in your bio encouraging the other.

Make sure to fill in as many of the 'about' information fields as possible to create depth and trust for prospects. We've all had 'friend' requests from random people with nothing on their profile, no education history or location, and hardly any photos. If so, I bet you don't jump at the chance to join a call of theirs – right? So don't fall into the same trap.

So, now you have optimised your profile for lead generation, it is time to hang out with your dream clients using the following tried and tested formulas.

1. Post once a day on your Facebook profile (not page)

In Step 4 (see page 77), I'll show you precisely what to post each day to gain maximum attendance at your Weekly Moment™.

In the meantime, remember that daily posting shows a busy profile when prospects from target groups check you out and fill their feed with value once they become friends.

2. Make five comments on other people's posts

Next, it is time to interact with people in your target groups.

Your game plan is to add value by helping other group members when they ask questions or by joining a conversation and giving your opinion.

Each day, set a target of commenting on five of your dream clients' posts.

You're essentially fishing for an opportunity, and the idea is to spark conversation, then move into Direct Messaging (DM) and ultimately move on to the next step in your funnel.

To handle the process, I recommend you adopt CLAM, a robust

system you can use for all your prospecting activity on social media (regardless of platform).

Here is how it works:

C is for Comment: Simply reply to someone's post (or their comment on someone else's post) with some value or encouraging words. For example, if they're discussing the best email marketing software, you could say:

> *"Hi [insert name], as you can see from the other comments, there are several options, but I'd recommend MailerLite as it has the most features for the lowest price. If you want to host online courses, run a website, and do email marketing on one platform, then Kajabi's probably best. I might be able to dig out a discount code for each of them if it helps?"*

The model above adds value and tempts prospects to jump into DMs to receive a discount code where you can offer to help even more.

L is for Like: Always 'liking' a comment and replying to it means your prospect will see you twice in their feed. It helps to prove you're interested, which makes them more likely to accept moving to the next stage.

A is for Add: There are two reasons to ask to 'friend' prospects. First, your message won't get filtered out as spam, which is essential for effective follow-up. Second, once a prospect has engaged with you, they are more likely to enjoy some of your other content – including, perhaps, your Weekly Moment™, promoted on your feed. As a new friend, they are also far more likely to see your new posts over the following days.

This tactic helps you to grow your email list, moving prospects further along your funnel, and fills your social network with potential clients waiting for your next post or event.

In short, it is a beautiful momentum-based tactic, as the more people who follow/friend you, the more engagement your posts receive, which leads to even more followers and opportunities.

M is for Message: After all three of the above, you can send a DM. To speed things up, you don't need to wait until your 'friend' request is accepted.

This method starts a conversation, the ultimate aim of which is to add value before moving prospects onto your email list. So, in the case of the example regarding the best email-marketing software above, you might message:

> *"Hi [insert name], as promised, I've dug out the discount codes. Let me have your email, and I'll send them across. I hope they help!*
>
> *I also have an email marketing event coming up, which I think will be right up your street, so I can send over some details for that. All the best, Richard."*

The above not only helps you move prospects from Facebook chat to email communication, but it also seeds attendance at your Weekly Moment™ – all while fulfilling your promise of help (the discount codes).

And you don't necessarily need discount codes: free eBooks, events, swipe files or checklists all work just as well.

3. Post one Trojan Horse each day

Now it's time to work with those five target groups I helped you find earlier!

Having a 'Monday Group', a 'Tuesday Group' etc., allows me to make sure I regularly generate conversation and interest in each group without looking like I'm spamming them, which is where the concept of a Trojan Horse comes in.

I'm sure you have all heard the story of the original Trojan Horse, which describes how – after a ten-year siege – Greek soldiers were eventually able to take the city of Troy by hiding inside a giant wooden horse left as an offering.

The following night inside the city, the Greek warriors emerged, opened the city gates and let in the rest of the Greek army, who subsequently took over the city.

It is a great story and a fascinating concept to apply to Facebook marketing.

Think about each of your target groups as a mini Troy and the administrators of each group as a guard waiting for you to make a wrong move – to try to sell a product, say, or plug an event – so they can kick you out.

Aim to use an offering to show you mean well.

The best form for your Trojan Horse is an engagement-creator post. Administrators of a group love it when members help with engagement (it means they have to do less to ensure the growth of the group). And, the higher your engagement statistics, the more people see the posts, and the more Facebook will suggest to others that they may like to join the group.

Your Trojan Horse, then, is a win/win.

However (enter sinister Greek warriors), don't just help that engagement by commenting back and enjoying the conversation. Instead, make a point of CLAM-ing everyone who engages, ensuring you create daily opportunities for your target groups.

Your engagement creator can be a poll, a question, a review of a product or service, or a request for a podcast or book recommendation – anything that drives comments and engagement.

Make sure you avoid being overly sales-y and mixing up the media. There's nothing like using a poll every time to make administrators suspicious.

Closing Thoughts

Now that you know how to find and hang out with your target audience on LinkedIn or Facebook and how that activity can generate leads, let's talk about expectations.

On average, our clients see 10-20 qualified leads per month. In some cases, it rises to over 30, but this tends to be for businesses with a strong value proposition and precise targeting.

However, you are also likely to generate a lot of connections who – whether through lousy timing or a simple lack of need – are not interested in your offer.

Never let this put you off, though – remember that LinkedIn and Facebook are social networks, not databases. In other words, each person gets to select the activity on their feed, and not all dream clients will be dream responders. Bear in mind, too, that a one-person consultancy might list themselves on LinkedIn as a company with 11-50 employees to look bigger than they are, or people might join Facebook groups without really being that interested in the subject.

So be prepared for some poor fits to slip through. However, with effective targeting and clear processes to verify that contacts are a good fit, you will find that most leads will be ideal prospects for your business.

Remember, too, that you'll need to invest a significant amount of time – approximately an hour a day to send out connection requests, respond to inbound leads, and filter through the good and bad fits. This 'to-do' list is why, once you've nailed the process and are seeing results, I recommend you use ads, automation and hire a lead-generation service or Virtual Assistant to do much of this legwork and scale your lead generation. (I return to these subjects in Steps 6 and 7, pages 161 and 167.) That way, you'll be free to spend 15-20 minutes per day nurturing the most promising leads.

Step 3
Move them into
your database

Now that you know your ideal client and how to find, connect, and build a conversation with them on social media, it is time to transfer them to a location where you own the communication stream.

An active email list is one of your best assets because it's part of your owned media i.e. media channels over which your business has complete control. Consequently, it is immune to sudden algorithm changes, has a far better reach than paid media, and is more cost-effective.

In this case, your list will take the form of an email database of subscribed target-audience members who you have permission to share your thought leadership with (and to continue to prospect with) away from social media.

Why is list building so important?

For every $1 spent on email marketing, the average expected return is $42, according to DMA Marketer Email Tracker. Compare this to the ROI of other channels, such as Pay-Per-Click advertising –

just $2 for every $1 spent – and it is clear that email marketing is a desirable – even imperative – channel.

No matter the size of your business, prospects on an email list are vital in shaping the success of your marketing campaigns. They are easy-to-track performance metrics (including open, click-through and conversion rates), which relay essential information about what you are getting right and what you might need to tweak.

How to get prospects onto your list

As we discussed in Step 2, a classic info swap is usually the best way to harvest connections from social media for your list.

In essence, an info-swap exchanges some value your Weekly Moment™, say, or an eBook, 5-day challenge or mini-course for a prospect's name, email, and even telephone number.

It makes moving prospects onto your list simple. For example, once you have established a connection, you can use questions such as:

"I noticed you were interested in [xyz]. We're running an event demonstrating how to do [xyz] and achieve [abc] in the process. Would you like me to send you an invite?" **[Event info-swap]**

"We helped [insert company name] achieve [xyz] and wrote up a case study that shows how we did it. Would you like me to send it to you?" **[Case-study info-swap]**

"I've written a book on [x]. It includes lessons I've learned from working with [name drop 2–4 other clients]. Would you like me to send you a copy?" **[eBook info-swap]**

"My company does [xyz]. Would you like to see our portfolio?" **[Portfolio info-swap]**

Then, whenever you receive a 'yes', you can casually reply:

"Great! What's your email? I'll send it straight over."

Never send something via the social feed. Your goal is to move the conversation to the more formal setting of your email inboxes and to add the prospect's details to your email marketing database. I strongly recommend using MailerLite or ActiveCampaign to manage your database; both are low-cost and user-friendly.

> **TIP:** Once your info swap works well, you can introduce the paid-ads tactics we cover in Step 6 to grow your database quickly.

Once you have added a prospect to your database, you can tag them as a new lead and move them from 'awareness' to 'consideration'.

First, you must close the loop on your social media chat. Conversations that remain on social media platforms tend to go nowhere; moving to email is a sign that leads are interested and want to find out more.

An excellent way to do this is to ask your lead to confirm they have received the info you sent (that way, you come across as attentive rather than pushy):

"Hi [insert first name], I know you won't have had time to review it yet, but I just wanted to double-check you received my email with [insert name of info-swap]. Thanks again."

Their reply will give you the opportunity, a day or so later, to continue the conversation by asking for feedback.

Once prospects have joined your email list, the 'awareness' stage is over, and you've successfully moved them to 'consider'.

It is your job to warm them up to book a sales appointment.

Collating your existing list

Many Sprinters who start working on lead generation are already sitting on a database of potential leads. Some are previous clients (you can find their details in your accounts system or email inbox); others might be prospects whom you have done little more than converse with, so far. Some might be Facebook or LinkedIn connections you haven't translated into a database yet, while others might be sitting on an old Mailchimp email list – or even in a dusty pile of business cards.

Now, then, is the moment to add them to your new, updated email list.

Much of the work we'll be doing in Step 4 needs you to have a list to work with, so collate as many names and emails as possible. You may be pleasantly surprised by how big your list is!

Step 4
Over-deliver value
for free pre-sale

Once a client is in your eco-system, you want them to binge on your content – and your tactic should be to help them do this as quickly as possible. The best way to achieve this is to throw a kitchen sink's worth of value at them while you're at the front of their mind.

Enter: The Weekly Moment™

The Weekly Moment™ is the focal point of your consideration activity. It is where marketing easily transitions into sales, and the customer experience is delivered in a value-driven non-sales-y way.

For most service-sector business owners, The Weekly Moment™ will be a short, weekly event delivered digitally which should take no longer than 45 minutes.

I highly recommend focusing on 13 events that you present on a weekly loop. Not only is 13 sufficient for your audience not to notice any repetition, but it also makes life more straightforward as it represents 52 weeks divided by four.

That way, your 13-week cycle will become a quarterly rhythm for marketing that can be optimised, perfected, automated, and delegated to your current or future marketing team to promote.

Each week, you'll invite new prospects, demonstrate value to them for the first part of the session (around 15-20 minutes). You will answer questions, give specific advice, and foster debate between the attendees for the remainder of the 45-minute session.

During the session – and then again, just before the last question– you, as the host, should offer sales-presentation slots (strategy sessions) to any attendee who wants to see how some of what you have covered will work specifically within their business.

Most Sprinters who use this system find that many prospects book strategy sessions directly into their diary before the weekly event is over. However, if some attendees need a further nudge, a follow-up set of emails and phone calls invariably yields the total volume of sales meetings from each session.

Each week, you should target 30 Weekly Moment™ registrations; in our experience, around 20 will show up, and your goal is to book five strategy sessions and close two of these into clients. Remember, though, these numbers are over the fullness of time; in general, a lead-to-sale conversion rate tends to take more than a week.

Also, if you sell a low- to medium-ticket item, you may need more than five strategy sessions and two sales to hit your income goals, in which case you will need to ratchet up your attendees. I'll return to this in more detail in Step 6. You can achieve this by using ads (if you're using Facebook for your awareness stage) or direct-message automation (if you're using LinkedIn).

The graph below will help to bring the process to life:

Graph 1: Client Weekly Moment™ registrations of 23

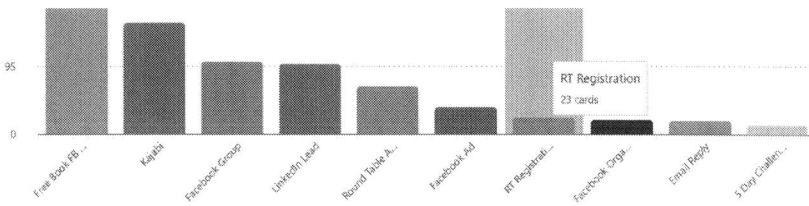

In this example, from 23 RT registrations, the event's founder could expect to achieve 16 attendees, three strategy sessions and one sale.

It is an exciting model, as effective paid ads and organic outreach strategy will scale attendees at your Weekly Moment™, and your sales volumes will scale with them.

For example, the funnel visualisation below is of a typical Weekly Moment™ system. Note the strategic communication leading up to events and the follow-up activity afterwards, designed to gain maximum participation from your database.

As this funnel can act as your 'one thing', providing maximum yield from your awareness and consideration activity, please be aware that this communication is essential.

Graph 2: Weekly Moment™ end-to-end funnel

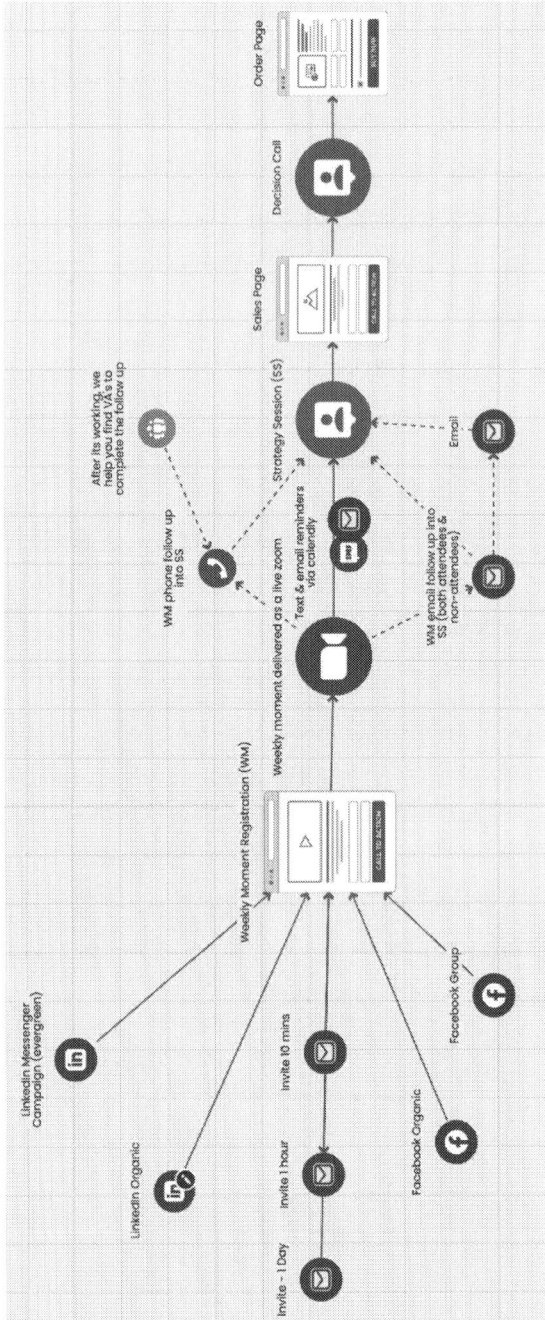

Don't run this funnel alongside another high-communication-based system, as you will end up over-communicating to your email database.

I recommend you make it your only funnel and instead go deep. Like miners, the deeper you go, the more gold you'll find!

Below is the definitive process to help you do just that.

Naming your Weekly Moment™ Series

As the Weekly Moment™ is a series of different events, an overarching name that is strong, focused, communicates the purpose of the series, and makes clear why prospects should attend, is vital.

Keep it simple, obvious, and incorporate your target audience name. Good examples include: 'The Construction Round Table', 'The Salon Owners' Forum' or 'The Project Managers' Network'.

Your goal is to make clients realise you're inviting them to an interactive event – rather than a webinar at which they'll receive a hard sell.

It would be best if you also found a balance between length and purpose, i.e. don't over-cram keywords, which will only compromise your name's overall effectiveness.

The Million Dollar Sprint's Weekly Moment™, for example, is: 'The Marketing Round Table'.

Although we considered 'The Service-Sector Entrepreneurs' Marketing Round Table' or 'The Million Dollar Sprint Marketing Round Table', short and sweet in the end won the day as we decided they were both too much of a mouthful.

As the umbrella for your 13-week cycle of 13 different but related event themes (peeled from your core offering, i.e. your flagship product), you also need to avoid your name being topic-specific.

For example, one of our event themes is 'Facebook Ads', which we can publicise by saying: "Attend the Marketing Round Table this week to deep dive into Facebook Ads."

> **Action 1:** Once you have a few ideas, create a poll in the Million Dollar Sprint™ community and ask your fellow Sprinters for feedback on the names you present. That way, you'll get a feel for what lands and why. If your ideas are not quite right, they'll help you reset off-piste thinking.

> **Action 2:** Once you have three or four good ideas, ask your target audience for their thoughts by running similar polls in Facebook groups or, if you prefer LinkedIn, set up a poll on your profile and ask for help from people in the right niche.

Carrying out both actions has two benefits: first, you'll receive great feedback from the people who matter; second, you'll seed the idea of the event in your audience's mind.

But remember to connect with and directly message everyone who votes to thank them. Not only is it polite, it also opens the communications channels and allows you to continue the conversation and invite them to the first event once you're ready to launch.

In other words, it is a great way to start prospecting immediately.

Branding your Weekly Moment™ system

Next, it is time to give your new-found name a brand. Indeed, it is critical if you want your Weekly Moment™ to feel professional and have longevity.

As each of your 13 events will need social media posts and headers that tie into each other, an overarching logo is essential. My advice when creating this is to keep it simple – and not spend a fortune.

> **TIP:** You can use Freelance Services Marketplace Fiverr.com, for example, to find a suitable designer and create a respectable-looking logo for around £30.

Once you have your logo, you will need to create the 13-week cycle of assets that links to it: Headers for your event pages on Facebook or LinkedIn, for example, or thumbnails for your replays if you're hosting them on YouTube, which I strongly recommend.

I'll return to this, but for now, remember that when you create your logo, it needs to work well alongside other designs.

Translating your 13 themes into Weekly Moment™ events

Now you have your umbrella brand, it is time to consider the names of your 13 sub-events.

The first step is to write down the themes of all 13 events. Remember, the most crucial factor is that they need to relate to your flagship product, i.e. the core offer you pitch to clients after each event.

Imagine your flagship product as an orange with 13 segments, each of which you'll unpeel into a theme that you can present as a slice of great content.

With just 15-20 minutes of presentation time, providing enough information for attendees to implement your ideas fully without further help is impossible. The beauty of the Weekly Moment™, then, is that it educates while creating more questions than answers. Questions such as: *"So how do I do that for my business?"*, *"What's the best way to start?"* and *"How much will it cost?"*

These are significant buying signals, so make sure your response is: *"Great question! But, as we're short on time, let's book a strategy session where I can walk you through the answer."*

The lead becomes a sales pitch, and the Weekly Moment's™ work is complete!

As an example, we used our Marketing Round Table to unpeel the following 13 event ideas from the Million Dollar Sprint Accelerator:

1. Facebook Ads

2. LinkedIn Organic

3. Trello

4. Flagship-Product Creation

5. Creating Demand

6. Email Marketing

7. Appointment Setting

8. Niche/Audience Targeting

9. Scaling to a Million in Revenue

10. Lead-Generation Basics

11. Facebook Groups

12. 5-Day Challenges

13. Staying Focused

Now it's your turn...

Create your list right now. But don't overthink it – titles will come next – simply scribble down 13 ideas.

1: _____

2: _____

3: _____

4: _____

5: _____

6: _____

7: _____

8: _____

9: _____

10: _____

11: _____

12: _____

13: _____

Jazzing up your 13 themes

Your event titles may be the most critical piece of your Weekly Moment™ marketing. You will reference them in every marketing email, social media post, direct message and advert.

As such, they need to communicate value and drive registrations.

To ensure you nail them, below are some easy-to-apply formulas that have led to success for your fellow Sprinters. All you need to do is find the right one, plug in the necessary details of your event, and BOOM! – you have a title that rocks. Make sure you use a blend of them, too many of one type can turn into white noise.

1. Lists

Formula: Ten Little-Known Ways to ____

Everyone likes a list, and lists give audiences a clear idea of what to expect from your event. But make sure your title is niche enough to attract your specific audience.

'Ten ways to be better at business', for example, is so general that it doesn't communicate value and isn't specific enough to target your niche audience.

More targeted list titles might include:

- Ten ways to use TikTok to increase conversions

- Five little-known habits of the most successful online entrepreneurs

- The top seven ways to increase brand awareness on Pinterest.

At Million Dollar Sprint™, we use:

- Six super-simple tactics for booking more sales appointments

- Eight steps to $1,000,000 in revenue.

2. How to …

Formula: How to do [_____] like [_____]

'How to' titles are a great way to show authority. Not only will you tell people how to do something, but you'll tell them how to do it like an expert. Attendees know they will leave your event with practical tips and actionable takeaways.

For example:

- How to promote your coaching business like a marketing pro

- How to structure your workday like Steve Jobs

- How to build your website like a professional coder.

At Million Dollar Sprint™, we use:

- How to create demand for what you do by limiting the supply of 'you'

- How to run a 5-day challenge like a sales Ninja

- How to run a Facebook group to get leads and make sales.

3. 101 …

Formula: [Interesting topic] 101: Learn How to [_____]

'101' titles may make your audience feel like beginners, but they also convey that your event will be chock-full of valuable information.

'101' titles are particularly great for covering new or trending topics, as they make it clear that even beginners will be able to understand the event's content.

For example:

- Product photography 101: Staging and lighting tips for beginners

- Instagram ads 101: From creating great ads to boosting click-through rates

- Web design 101: How to create clean, high-converting websites.

At Million Dollar Sprint™, we use:

- Lead-generation 101: For service businesses.

4. Classes, Training, and Workshops

Formula: [Event topic] [Masterclass/Workshop/Training]

Unlike 101-titles, the use of the words 'masterclass', 'training' or 'workshop' communicates that your event will include in-depth information. Typically, these events are not for beginners (unless you explicitly state this), and attendees will expect to gain exclusive knowledge from industry leaders.

For example:

- Advanced Pinterest workshop: Staying ahead of algorithm updates

- eCommerce masterclass for small B2B businesses

- Mobile SEO Training: Keywords and content strategy.

At Million Dollar Sprint™, we use:

- LinkedIn organic lead-generation masterclass.

5. New ...

Formula: New data reveals how [your target audience] should be doing [_____]

Titles that include – or imply – the word 'new' are exciting and timely. Audiences are attracted to them because they suggest they'll receive exclusive information most people don't yet have access to.

It is a great way to create urgency and convey that your brand is current and relevant.

For example:

- New techniques to boost your wealth mindset

- New Facebook strategies to attract more likes and followers

- New technology all yoga instructors should know about.

At Million Dollar Sprint™, we use:

- Trello's the reason for our rapid growth: Let me show you why.

6. Trends

Formula: The new trend in [_____] that [add benefit]

Trending titles/topics are a great way to involve yourself in more significant conversations and to show your audience you are aware of the latest industry developments.

Attendees expect a fresh perspective, so you can use trending events to position yourself as an industry expert, sharing forward-thinking views and thought-provoking content.

For example:

- Video-ad trends: Changing the way we connect with brands

- Smartphone trends: Are they worth the upgrade?

- Natural-living trends: They'll have you seeing green.

At Million Dollar Sprint™, we use:

- The top marketing trends for [enter year ahead].*

We run this as a pop-up event twice a year, which we usually slot into our 13-week cycle in the second week of December and at the start of January to ensure we hit our audience at the right time with on-trend content. Never be afraid to do this whenever new trends appear in your market – the 13 weeks are always flexible.

REMEMBER: However unique your event's content is, if the name doesn't grab your audience's attention, they're unlikely to see it. Our foolproof formulas will ensure a boost in registrations and attendance rates.

Now it's your turn...

Read through the formulas again, then use them to jazz up your 13 themes into eye-catching event names below:

1: _____

2: _____

3: _____

4: _____

5: _____

6: _____

7: _____

8: _____

9: _____

10: _____

11: _____

12: _____

13: _____

Timing your Weekly Moment™

Alongside name and brand, the time you host your weekly event is also key to capturing your audience. In general, these are the four optimum times:

1. **9 am**: As it is the first work appointment of the day for most prospects, it is the least likely to be disrupted by other events that happen to them during the day, which means the show-up rate is always strong.

2. **'Lunch & Learn'**: Ideal for corporate or direct-to-consumer prospects as they can jump on the call during a break in their schedule.

3. **4 pm or 5 pm** – i.e. the last hour of the working day: Clients can complete their workday and make your event their last activity. It is perfect for parents, too, as they can do the school run, get their kids settled, and then jump in.

4. **7 pm (or even 8 pm)**: If you live in the EU, this is perfect for an international audience as it works for the USA and Australasia. If you do not live in the EU, you'll need to adjust the timings.

Make sure you book your first Weekly Moment™ at least two weeks in advance (perhaps three if this is your first introduction to the system). This gap will give you time during the first week to outline your presentation, circulate a launch email and set up all the necessary elements.

That way, the week of the event itself, all you'll need to do is follow the system that I will outline in the weekly rhythm section of this book. It includes three promotional emails and a daily social media post, all designed to ensure you get bookings.

Now it's your turn...

Select the time slot best for your target market; you could even ask them using a poll just as you did for your brand, then create a recurring slot in your diary for your new Weekly Moment™.

Before you move on, make sure you write the day and time below, so it's logged in your plan:

Weekly Moment™ day of the week:

_____

Weekly Moment™ start time:

_____

Your Call to Action (CTA)

The design of the Weekly Moment™ is to help prospects consider you before moving into the conversion stage.

Your CTA, then, is for prospects to book a strategy session with you at which you can pitch your flagship product. The agenda and script below will show you how best to present this opportunity to them.

NOTE: Some Sprinters may opt to sell directly at their Weekly Moment™, which gives the events more of a webinar format. This choice is usually when their offering is low- to mid-ticket, and prospects can decide to join and pay then and there.

Your Weekly Moment™ Agenda

Total Length: 45 minutes

The aim is to leave your audience wanting more. (In other words, short and snappy wins the race.)

That said, an excellent way to over-deliver is to book an hour in your diary and then if the Q&A section is going well, you can always spend an extra 5-10 minutes squeezing in a few more questions.

Part 1: Small Talk (3 minutes)

Please make a point of opening the door dead on your start time and call each person by name as they come in. This individual recognition is vital to making your audience feel welcome and part of the meeting.

It also encourages attendees to keep their video on – human nature being what it is, being both seen and welcomed will make them feel obliged to participate more actively.

Next, let the audience know you're looking for a fun anecdote, a win, or something of interest while you wait for everyone to filter in. Be sure to set a time limit to avoid any rambling and the loss of precious time with your audience.

For example: *"Morning everyone, I'm just letting the room filter in, then we'll start about three minutes past nine. In the meantime, who has an interesting anecdote or story from their week?"*

Part 2: Housekeeping & Agenda (2 minutes)

You might, for example, let the audience know the session is recorded and remind them that you'd love to see lots of questions in the chat, which you will answer as you go or at the end.

Once you've done this – and I would recommend keeping the same housekeeping rules each week, so your audience gets used to them – you can move to the day's agenda.

Put this on a slide and make it super simple with just two parts: 1: The name of the day's event; 2: Q&A.

Remind them again that you've left plenty of time for questions; as – as the meeting is a Round Table/Discussion Forum, audience participation is the name of the game.

Part 3: Value (15-20 minutes)

This section is your time to shine, but keep it short to one or two large-value bombs. Never over-deliver – less is more.

The topic should help or inspire your audience and, as a result, create plenty of discussion points for the Q&A section.

If you over-deliver in this section, I tend to find that you blow people's minds and leave them overwhelmed without the head space to ask good questions.

Make sure you don't reference your CTA at this point – your aim is to move straight into the Q&A and get the audience livened up.

Part 4: Q&A (20-25 minutes)

This final section will roll to the end. The skill lies in getting that all-important first question from your audience and then using it to create a profound answer that you can link back to your content where possible, to ensure it stays relevant.

Once you have answered this first question, the next step is to make the first reference (of three) to your CTA – in this case, to your strategy session.

For example, you might say something along these lines:

"Thank you for your question, [their name]. Before I take the next question, I just wanted to mention if anything I've covered today resonates in any way. Let's jump on a strategy session together if you'd like to spend some time with me individually to run through how it applies to your specific situation and business.

It's a value-packed session, but I only have a limited number of seats each week, so if you're interested, jump on the booking link I've just added to the chat.

Can you all see it? [Yes'] Great, give it a click to grab your slot now."

As you say this, ensure you share your screen to show what happens when they click the booking link. Visualise the process for them and explain it – you want them to be booking as you do. For example:

"Simply go to the calendar and grab one of the limited time slots you now see. But be quick as they get booked up fast – other sessions also use it to book time into my diary.

And remember, at the end of your strategy session, we'll have created a plan on how you can get to [XYZ result]."

At this point, you could even introduce a slide which goes through the three or four bullet-point benefits of attending a strategy session before you go back to gallery view and return to the Q&A by saying:

"OK, great, I look forward to spending more time with you then ... Right, who's next with a question?"

The second time you mention your CTA will be just three minutes or so from the end of the session:

"I'll take a question now from [their name], but before I do, I just wanted to re-post the booking link and remind everyone about the strategy sessions when we can go through some of the ideas from today together and create a plan for you to get [XYZ result].

Jump on it quickly, though, as I've received a few pings on my phone, which means some of you have already booked, so the availability of the limited slots will be getting less by the minute."

Mentioning the 'pings' on your phone creates social proof, while referring to the limited number of sessions establishes the idea of scarcity, both of which will encourage anyone sitting on the fence to take action and book. You don't even need to check your phone – presume that some people will have booked instantly.

The final reference to your CTA should simply be:

"OK, thank you for a fantastic round table. I'm going to wrap up now, but I look forward to seeing some of you in a strategy session soon. Have a great day!"

Now it's your turn...

First, download the Weekly Moment™ Agenda from our online portal, then tailor it to reflect your business and CTA. I don't recommend you read directly from this, but having the exact words you want to use written out in front of you as a reminder before your first couple of events is a great way to cement them into your natural flow.

Next, download our Weekly Moment™ presentation-slides template. The slides tie into the agenda and – by acting as prompts – make sure you cover all the elements as you go through each session.

TIP: If you don't already have your own booking software, Calendly [https://calendly.com/] is good – it's super easy to use and has a nice visual.

Finally, to see how I close an audience into booking a strategy session, you can watch all the Million Dollar Sprint's Weekly Moments™ – The Marketing Round Table – on our YouTube channel here: www.youtube.com/c/RichardWoods

What Technology Should You Use?

To avoid overcomplicating life, I recommend using the same tool to harvest registrations for your Weekly Moment™ events as you do to host them.

In most instances (due to its low cost and mass uptake), this will be Zoom, where attendees can register directly on the event webpage it generates.

If you look at the example, you'll note that we've set ours up so that attendees register for all the events in the series (i.e. for however long you've set the recurring-meeting setting). As a guide, I always extend mine for a year, then open it again for another year when I get to December.

The beauty of Zoom is that you can ask for attendees' names and request their email and phone number (or any other details you might need), which you can use for event reminders and follow-up activities.

The only downside of using a recurring event like the one in the example is that as your event changes each week, your booking page doesn't – it is impossible to be subject-specific. This is why promoting your 13-week cycle is vital – it lets prospects know the focus of each event, and that there are similar events each week, in which they can participate.

As a bonus, Zoom allows you to edit the confirmation emails automatically sent to new registrations. You can link to extra-value content for attendees to watch before the event if they wish.

On the day of the event itself, Zoom has a couple of applicable settings that will help you manage your audience. The first is to allow a waiting room so you can double-check people on the way in to make sure you're happy with them; the second is to enable you to opt out of automatically recording the event. Instead, start recording once the room has filtered in (it saves a lot of time later as you won't need to edit before you upload and share the event).

Now it's your turn...

Set up your recurring Weekly Moment™ Zoom meeting and registration page.

Your First Weekly Moment™: Launch Timeline

Two Weeks Out

As I mentioned, starting at least two weeks out gives you plenty of time to focus on naming and branding, including posting your 'What shall I call it?' poll to start warming up your target audience.

One Week Out

One week before, announce the focus of your first event by referring to your 13-week cycle, selecting Week 1's topic and posting it on LinkedIn or Facebook, and sending out a launch email to your audience.

This email is in addition to the three you'll send as a regular part of every event's weekly process. It is unique to 'launch week' and specifically designed to attract the first wave of attendees.

Keep it friendly and straightforward, though, along the lines below which you can also repurpose into a social media post to promote your launch to an even wider audience:

Dear [first name],

We're delighted to announce that next Wednesday at 9 am, we'll launch our first [name of Weekly Moment™] event.

The [name of Weekly Moment™] is designed specifically for [target audience] who are looking to [specific pain you solve].

Each week we'll focus on a different segment of [specific pain you solve], giving you the best advice from a team who've all been there and got the T-shirt.

Our BIG FOCUS next Wednesday is [title of event], and I'll walk you through, step-by-step, how to [add some benefits of their attending].

I hope you agree it's an eye-catching event, so join me for just 45 minutes of high-quality training and discussion next Wednesday at 9 am.

Register for one of our limited seats by CLICKING HERE.

Best regards

[your email signature]

The Week of the First Event

All the work you've put into your 13-week cycle starts to pay off. And the benefit of pre-planning your daily promotional rhythm is that in this first week you do not need to do anything special; simply follow each of the daily steps.

Remember that our model works on consistency and growth, so don't put too much pressure on yourself. If you only get a few bookings and attendees this first week, don't worry – it is a great place from which to build.

The Weekly Moment™ Recording

To enable fast and effective follow-up, you should share the event recording as quickly as possible with attendees and any other parties you feel would be interested.

YouTube is best for sharing. Unlike other social networks such as LinkedIn, Instagram and TikTok, it doesn't limit the length of videos you can upload and has a potent search-engine tool. It will also ensure other potential clients see your content.

Consistent posting of new content each week will build your channel and audience (a particular win/win considering that YouTube is free). In addition, hosting all your replays openly on one platform means that any potential clients you direct to one of your replays will have the opportunity to gorge on all your previous sessions. Of course, the aim is to confirm your expertise and, ultimately, inspire them to work with you.

Although it's not vital to start with, to make your channel look more professional (and the video itself more 'clickable'), further along the line, I would recommend including a thumbnail image for each video.

The simplest way to do so is by asking your designer (remember Fiverr.com?) to produce 13 YouTube thumbnails alongside the 13 event headers and social media posts you use to promote the event.

I will go into more detail on this later, but for now, note that briefing a designer to produce a package of designs for *all* the events in your 13-week cycle is the best way to optimise your budget (it means you can ask for a bulk deal), and their time. And an added bonus is that seeing these all laid out together will inspire you to commit to the rhythm.

Sprinters ask me if they should upload each new cycle's content to YouTube, and my answer is always 'Yes'. This is because

i) it is impossible to deliver a live event precisely the same way every 14 weeks;

ii) the Q&A section will be different.

I advise changing the title and thumbnail so that each repetition looks different. If, for example, the title of your event in week 1 is 'A Beginner's Guide to Meditations', for cycle 2, you could change it to 'Meditation 101 – All You Need to Know', and for cycle 3, 'How to Fast-Track your Start to Meditation'. The good news is, you don't need to edit the emails associated with your 13-week cycle.

> **TIP:** Remember the power of ONE. YouTube is not your one way of driving traffic (awareness), so you don't need to spend hours on it. Simply use it as a video-sharing tool for your replays, and consider additional views of your content as a bonus.

> **Now it's your turn...**
>
> Set up your YouTube channel ready to start posting your Weekly Moment™ recordings.

Weekly Moment™ Follow-up

Once you've finished your Weekly Moment™, you will no doubt want to jump straight to your inbox to see how many scheduled strategy sessions are booked. However, although these represent your quick wins, the work certainly doesn't stop there. Now is the time to extract as much juice from the weekly squeeze as possible.

In a typical week, half of my strategy session bookings will come from the work *after* the live event, so remember: The fortune is in the follow-up.

Completing the following tasks will lead to the highest volume of strategy sessions booked and the increased sales that follow, so start by prioritising follow-up with the hottest prospects – your attendees – via a primary email and then a nudge two days later. (See diagram below.)

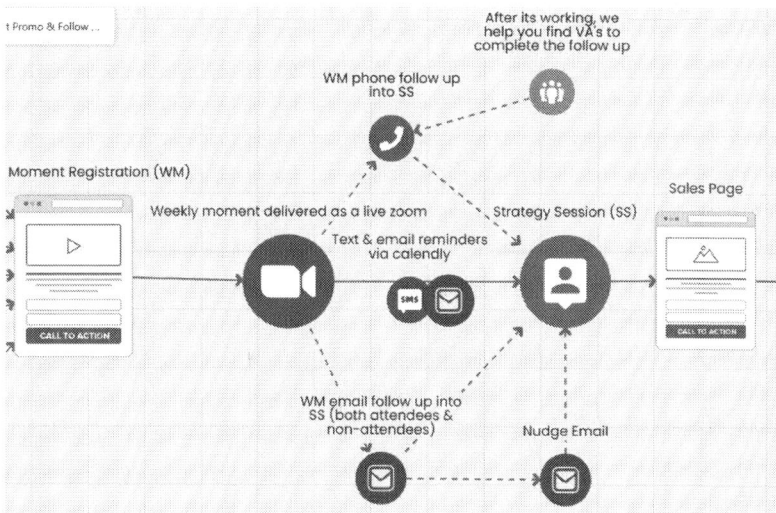

First Follow-up Email

The first email is the most important, and is composed of three elements:

1. A link to your Weekly Moment™ replay on YouTube

2. You can quickly pull together swipe files, cheat sheets, slides, tick lists, or bonus content. You could save the slides and notes you made when preparing the session as a PDF handout. Your audience will learn that you are an expert who delivers quality and is generous. That way, they'll want to continue learning from you, which positions you to ask for element 3.

3. Your call to action. Remember, this is why you created your Weekly Moment™. So take the opportunity to make a big statement that links the value prospects received at the event with the promise of even more – this time tailored to their specific situation – at a strategy session.

Here is an example template you might like to follow:

Email Title: Great to see you at the [event name]

Email Body:

Hi [first name],

I was delighted to see you at the [Weekly Moment] yesterday.

I hope the presentation was of value, and I wanted to forward these additional resources:

1. The swipe file: [name of document].

2. The replay of the training so you can recap it at your leisure: [YouTube link].

I'd also like to invite you to a strategy session to work through tactics like the ones I demonstrated yesterday, along with many other growth ideas for your business.

The strategy sessions are limited in number and not open to everyone, so do take me up on this offer if you're serious about growing your business.

Click here to BOOK THE STRATEGY SESSION now, and I look forward to spending more quality time with you.

Have a great day,

[your email signature]

To get the maximum bang for your buck, keep it personal by ensuring the emails come from you – as the event presenter – rather than one of your team, even if they create and manage the actual sending. (To make life easier, I have a second email – richard@milliondollarsprint.com – which my team manage and uses for me.)

Manually sending emails to each attendee has the added benefit of avoiding spam filters. And, as we're only targeting 20-30 attendees each week, the 15 minutes it takes to copy and paste their names and emails into the template isn't a huge burden when you consider the positive impact it has on bookings.

Second Follow-up Email: The Nudge

The idea of the nudge – which you should only send if you don't get a response to your first email – is to show that you are genuinely interested in meeting them again. You also feel and believe it is important enough to follow up as you know you can make a difference in their business.

The nudge email should be short and significant on the strategy session booking – nothing else.

Below is a helpful template to follow:

Email Title: A quick check-in [first name]

Email Body:

Hi [first name],

It was nice to see you at the [event name].

I trust you got some insights.

I wanted to reach out as I have two ideas to share that would significantly impact your business.

Are you available next Tuesday at 2 pm or Thursday morning for a catch-up?

Thanks,

[your email signature]

There are several things to note in this email. First, how specific it is. By saying: *"I have two extra ideas I'd like to share that I feel would make a big difference to your business"*, you have generated intrigue and emphasised that you are offering them an opportunity to learn more from you.

Second, rather than resending the booking link, I offer two specific dates, which – because it looks more authentic and as if you've specifically checked your availability – is more likely to elicit a response. However, always be mindful of speed in any follow-up system. You don't need to check your diary physically; send the exact times each week and work it out once you get a reply. If it turns out you're not available, it will simply serve to reinforce you are in demand. And, if neither of the dates you suggest works for the recipient, you can always send a link next time when the nudge email's work – to get the prospect talking to you – is done.

Finally, I purposely keep things loose by asking for a 'catch up' (rather than a 'strategy session'), which helps to calm anyone who is worried they might be booking onto a sales pitch. Although once they do book, the link clearly states 'strategy session', and you'll host it like any other.

> **TIP 1:** When you send a nudge email, do so by replying to your first email to create a chain. That way, it's easier for potential clients to reread your first email if they want to dig deeper.

> **TIP 2:** Whenever you get a response from follow-up emails, update your CRM and/or email list with the new information and remove any dead leads.

Weekly Moment™ Follow-up to Non-Attendees

As you're creating a new event each week, you'll find you have leads at different temperatures:

1. **Red-hot Leads** – who've booked a strategy session

2. **Hot Leads** – who've attended a Weekly Moment™

3. **Warm Leads** – who've booked (but not yet attended) a Weekly Moment™

4. **Lukewarm Leads** – who've participated in your content through an engagement creator, for example, or via a replay request (more on these below).

Make sure you actively follow up on all your leads at each stage when your goal is to move them to the next level – ideally fast-tracking as many as possible straight to a strategy session.

At stage one, you're presenting leads with your service to make a sale.

At stage two, leads will receive the two follow-up emails we've just covered.

At stages three and four, leads are potential prospects who haven't yet attended a Weekly Moment™ – which is exciting as it represents a whole wave of untapped opportunities for you to go after!

Stage 3: Warm Leads

This group of prospects were interested enough to register for your Weekly Moment™ and share their name, email, and phone number, yet they missed it.

You will usually have no idea why, but we all know life has a habit of getting in the way of our best intentions sometimes, so make sure you still treat them as great opportunities.

The best way of doing so is by sending them follow-up emails that – except for a few minor details – are almost the same as those you send to attendees.

For example, instead of "great to see you", you might say, "sorry I missed you". In other words, the email would look like this:

Email Title: Sorry we missed you [first name]

Email Body:

Hi [first name],

We had an amazing [Weekly Moment] yesterday, and I was sorry not to see you.

I understand plans change, though, so I've created these additional resources for you:

1. The swipe file: [name of document].

2. The replay of the training so you can recap it at your leisure: [YouTube link].

I'd also like to invite you to a strategy session to work through tactics like the ones I demonstrated yesterday, along with many other growth ideas for your business.

The strategy sessions are limited in number and not open to everyone, so do take me up on this offer if you're serious about growing your business.

Simply click here to BOOK THE STRATEGY SESSION now, and I look forward to spending quality time with you.

Have a great day,

[your email signature]

You can then similarly tweak your nudge email as well:

Email Title: A quick catch up [first name]

Email Body:

Hi [first name],

I just wanted to check in and see what you thought of the [event name] replay and swipe file?

I hope they delivered some insights.

I also wanted to reach out as I have two ideas I'd like to share that would make a big difference to your business.

Are you available next Tuesday at 2 pm or Thursday morning for a catch-up?

Thanks,

[your email signature]

Together, these emails should help generate an extra one or two strategy sessions a week from non-attendees, which – when your total weekly target is five – makes it a great tactic and well worth a little extra effort.

Stage 4: Lukewarm Leads

Lukewarm leads show up in two key areas:

1. Engagement creators
2. Replay requests.

Engagement Creators: I will be covering these in more detail later, but, as a brief overview, these are the big-picture questions or polls designed to get people talking (hence the name!) around the theme of each of your Weekly Moment™ events a couple of days in advance. As good engagement creators help filter your audience into a mainly engaged segment, they are pure gold.

Once prospects have engaged with a post, you can invite them to your Weekly Moment™ event. Then, when it is over, you can check back in to message anyone who didn't register and, therefore, would not have received the replay link and associated documents through stages 1, 2 and 3. Don't forget that warming up as many people as possible leads to a larger, more engaged audience.

If you receive a positive response, don't just send the replay link and additional resources via a social media message. Ensure you ask for their email address, add it to your database and invite them to your next event. As discussed in Step 3, the more extensive your list, the better your chance of hitting larger sales volumes.

Replay Requests: In our recommended sequence of hosting Weekly Moments™ on Wednesdays, you should schedule your 'Who wants the replay?' post for the day after, i.e. Thursday.

Here's one I've used:

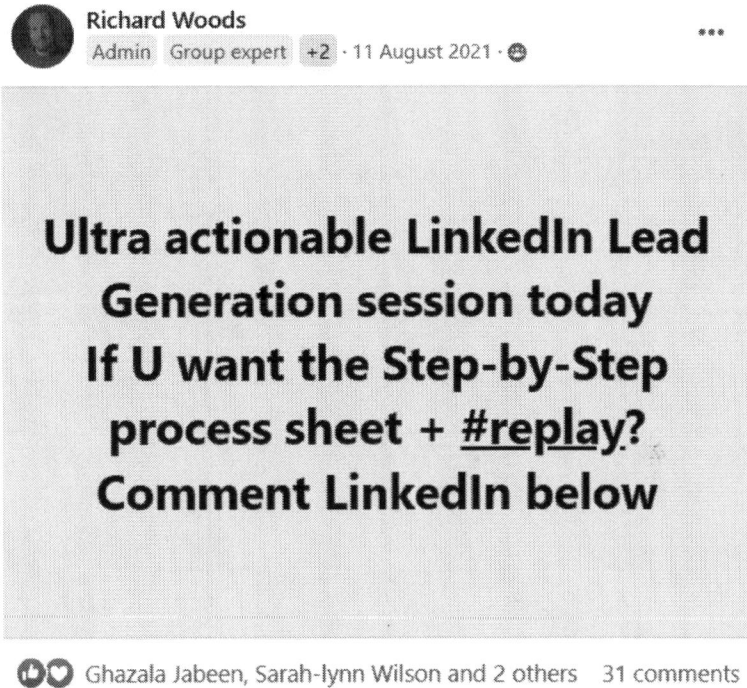

Ultra actionable LinkedIn Lead Generation session today If U want the Step-by-Step process sheet + #replay? Comment LinkedIn below

Ghazala Jabeen, Sarah-lynn Wilson and 2 others   31 comments

To make your post stand out, use a large font, an intense colour or an image of the session/ screenshot of the swipe file as a background. You can even include a video in which you explain some of the session's highlights and ask who would like the complete replay and swipe file.

As you can see, the few minutes' work it took me to write the post produced an extra 35 opportunities – it received four likes and 31 comments – to invite prospects to a strategy session.

On the following pages are some other examples of ways to increase engagement and build an audience of prospects who want to learn from you:

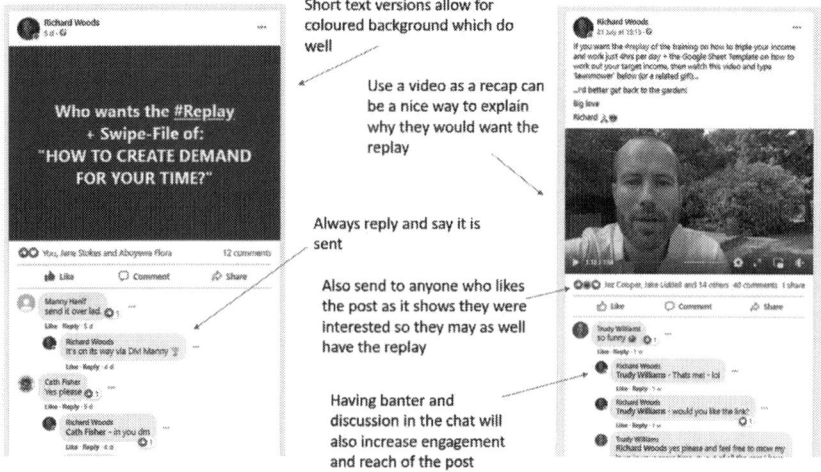

So, now you've caught a prospect's eye and inspired engagement, the next step is to handle the replies.

For the most success, I recommend you adopt the CLAM system we discussed in Step 2; for ease of reference, here is a reminder:

C is for Comment: Reply to their original comment saying, "It's on its way via DM". But make sure you mix up your responses slightly. The same reply repeatedly looks robotic to your audience (which can affect your authenticity) and to Facebook or LinkedIn (which can affect your reach, as the platform algorithms may think you're a bot).

L is for Like: Remember, 'liking' a comment and replying means your prospect will see you twice in their feed. It helps to prove you're interested, which makes them more likely to move to the next stage.

A is for Add: Asking to connect with or to 'friend' someone helps avoid spam filters, grows your network and promotes future engagement.

M is for Message: Congratulations – it is time for a direct message (DM). Each week, send a slightly tailored message to those who request the replay based on the following:

Hi [first name], I've just seen your replay and swipe file request. What's your email so I can send them over?

Once they reply, add them to your database, so they will get future event invites, and then send a follow-up email (and a nudge email, too, if appropriate) similar to those you sent to your hot and warm leads:

Email Title: [event name] Swipe File & Replay

Email Body:

Hi [first name]

Thank you for reaching out to [insert name of the platform] for the replay and resources. I've attached the following for you:

1. The swipe file: LinkedIn Lead-Generation Process & Outreach Templates.

2. The replay of the training [add YouTube link] so you can watch it at your leisure.

I'd also like to invite you to our Million Dollar Strategy Session to work through tactics like the LinkedIn one above, along with many other growth ideas for your business.

The strategy sessions are limited in number and not open to everyone, so do take me up on this offer if you're serious about growing your business.

BOOK STRATEGY SESSION

Have a great day,

[your email signature]

TIP: Once you have their email address, don't forget to add it to your database and prospect management system/pipeline. You've worked hard to create these leads, so make sure they are all followed up effectively and progressed into a strategy session – even the lukewarm ones

Your Social Rhythm

Now that you've decided on your themes for your Weekly Moment™ and have your 13 weeks in place, it is time to set up a social media schedule that drives registration and – ultimately – strategy session bookings.

What and how often you post on social media is your social rhythm.

Over the years, I have listened to, watched, read and – most importantly – tested countless statements regarding optimal posting frequencies.

But, having run campaigns for hundreds of clients with my lead-generation agency, I quickly learnt the magic formula for service-sector businesses based on the following four proven fundamentals:

1. Consistency is more important than frequency

2. *Quality* is more important than quantity

3. Yesterday dictates the success of today

4. Themes are your friend.

Bearing in mind that social media platforms reward 'dwell time' (how long someone looks at your post) and engagement signals (likes and shares) more than how much you post, let's expand on these fundamentals.

1. Consistency is more important than frequency

The main problem with suggesting posting frequencies is the lack of data. For instance, does the location of you and your audience affect posting? If so, how? Do different industries react differently to the number of posts you share? And, most importantly, what is your specific goal on social media?

A better alternative is to aim for consistency –making life easier as you need to create a plan and stick to it.

For example, deciding to post once a day means you know in advance that you need to create or curate enough content to meet that target, while your audience will see that they can visit your page every day and find fresh content.

2. Quality is more important than quantity

Remember, longer dwell time and higher engagement means your content will appear in your audience's newsfeed more often. So, if you want more people to see it, you must ensure your content is consistently high quality.

There is only one thing worse than not posting on social media: posting something that's not relevant or appropriate. Filling your audience's feed with poor-quality content and random noise will turn them off. In the search to refine my feed, I know I certainly unfollow as many people as I follow these days.

The best way to create relevant social media content is to focus on helpfulness and authenticity.

Simply put, you want your posts to make sense to the person engaging with them.

And never forget that *everything* you post reflects you and your brand. Do I want to see my trainer posting pictures from the kebab shop late on a Saturday night, for example?

It doesn't mean you need to drop a knowledge bomb every time you post; some of the best content is often a funny meme or a silly poll. Sometimes, you might post an aspirational photo or quote or upload a poll to spike interaction and debate. Remember, high dwell time and/or high engagement – likes, comments and shares – are your North Star.

3. Yesterday dictates the success of today

Social networks reward dwell time and engagement by boosting the reach of your original post, but they also presume your next post will be good, too – and very kindly give it a bit of a head start. (This is one reason why influencers seem to be everywhere.)

That's why I coined the concept of the 'alley-oop' social media post system.

In basketball, an alley-oop is an attacking play in which one player throws the ball to a teammate near the basket who jumps, catches it in mid-air, and slam dunks it before touching the ground again. (If you've never seen one, Google it now!)

To apply the concept to social media, you can use one day's post to tee up (to continue the sporting analogies!) the next. If, for example, you have a funny meme or high-engagement question, post it the day before a post that you want your audience to act on (i.e. by signing up for your Weekly Moment™).

In other words, the 'alley' is your high-engagement post, and the 'oop' is your conversion post leading to the slam dunk result of an increased number of Weekly Moment™ attendees.

4. Themes are your friend

At my lead-generation agency, a significant change we made for all our clients was to theme every day of the week: 'Engagement-Creator Monday', for example, or 'Share-a-Win Friday'. That way, we knew what post to send on any given day.

Knowing Friday was the day we shared client wins or testimonials, our team ensured we always had a good stock of high-quality posts that met this remit. We used a video or a screenshot of a client review – to schedule them months in advance.

Your 13-week cycle, which runs four times yearly, calls for a content calendar of 52 weekly themes. So, once your focus is locked in, you're ready to use the four fundamentals of your social media rhythm to develop a daily plan.

Applying the four fundamentals

Although you can host your Weekly Moment™ on any day of the week, choosing a **Wednesday** allows you to spend two days building up and two days following up.

We also know that the day after your Weekly Moment™ is about the replay, which means **Thursday** is your 'Who wants the replay?' day.

Below, then, is an outline of the remaining days:

Monday: This is the most critical day to spike your platform's algorithm and your reach, which makes Monday Engagement Creator day.

Tuesday: Remember our 'alley-oop' system? That means Tuesday is the day to promote your Weekly Moment™.

Friday: To grow your credibility each week, make Friday your 'Share a Win' day when you post testimonials and client results. I recommend you make it a two-post day and use it to tee up the following week's event. The most straightforward way is by using LinkedIn and Facebook's event modules to schedule a 'What's on Next Week' post.

Weekend: Saturday and Sunday are opportunities to relax and reveal your personality. This also serves to refresh the feed so you can go again next week with your next theme.

The diagram below illustrates a typical week, with the higher bars representing your desired peaks of audience engagement.

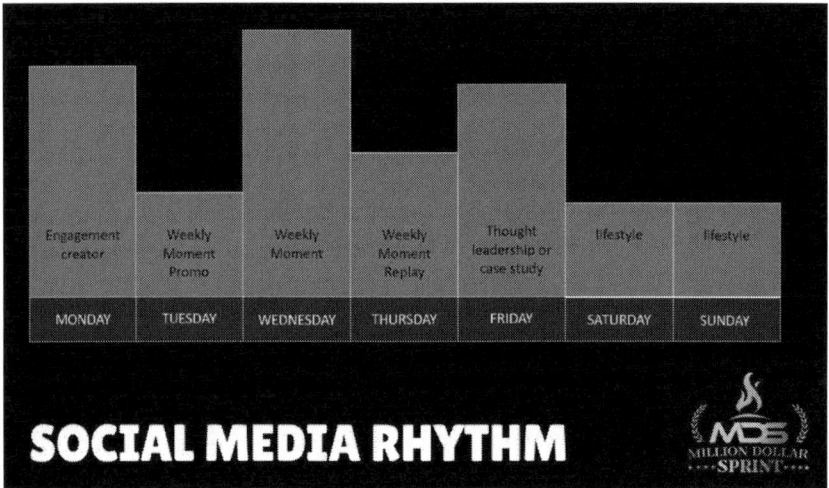

| Engagement creator | Weekly Moment Promo | Weekly Moment | Weekly Moment Replay | Thought leadership or case study | lifestyle | lifestyle |
| MONDAY | TUESDAY | WEDNESDAY | THURSDAY | FRIDAY | SATURDAY | SUNDAY |

SOCIAL MEDIA RHYTHM

Let's Go Deeper

As we have already covered the Wednesday Weekly Moment™ and the Thursday Replay posts in-depth, let's now drill down into the process for the other days.

Monday: Engagement Creator

As outlined above, this forms an essential part of your social media mix, using high-engagement style posts to spike the platform's algorithm and prime the reach of the rest of your content.

In other words, what better way to start the week?

Not only does deploying this tactic kick-start your week, but it is also the day before you send out the invites to your Weekly Moment™, which gives your Tuesday Call to Action post the best possible leg-up.

When approaching engagement creators, start by zooming out and focusing on your objectives. If you're going to get a ton of prospects interacting with your post, then you need to make sure it is related to your Call to Action.

In the case of our 13-week cycle, the objective is clear: For people to register for the Weekly Moment™.

Your engagement creator needs to tie in with the theme of the following Weekly Moment™. That way, you can thank everyone who engages in their interest and invite them to register for the event to find out more.

There are a few formats that do well. One of the most obvious is a poll or survey that prospects can vote on as they scroll through their feed.

In our experience, the simpler the options, the better – straightforward yes/no polls usually elicit the most interactions. Remember, you are aiming for a volume of engagement, not depth of survey data. The more engagement, the more leads you have to invite to your Weekly Moment™. Incidentally, although it's easy to post a poll on LinkedIn, it's a little trickier on Facebook as you can only do so through groups. However, as long as you have been paying attention, this shouldn't be a deal-breaker as we have already discussed the importance of using Facebook groups and Trojan Horse posts as a tool for success.

A second successful format is that of a short open question. If your Weekly Moment™ is 'How to become a published author', for example, you might ask, 'If you were to write a book, what would it be on?'

Whereas a poll is locked-down and quantitative – your audience is simply ticking pre-set opinions – this format is designed to result in more qualitative answers. And the beauty of this is that it helps to open their minds, so they start to include more information in their responses.

To inspire, I've listed examples below that you can apply equally well to either format. But remember, questions are pointless unless they relate to your Weekly Moment™ so consider this as a starting point only – you will need to tailor each query to your specific event and/or industry.

Examples

1. If you could wave a magic wand, where would your business be 12 months from now?

2. What is the best business-related film or documentary you have seen recently?

3. What is your favourite business podcast?

4. What job would you be terrible at?

5. What are you reading this week?

6. What are you listening to this week?

7. What are you interested in that most people haven't heard of?

8. How do you relax after a hard day's work?

9. What is the most annoying question people ask you?

10. What is the best thing that happened to you last week?

Work the engagement

So what happens once you have posted your engagement creator? First, I would recommend you immediately vote/answer the question, then add a comment in the chat. For example, you might say something like: *"I'm looking forward to seeing how this poll goes – I think [xyz], but it's a tough one to call because of [abc]."*

The idea is that by sharing your thoughts first, you'll spike comments and interactions from other people and build deeper conversations with them. And remember, the more interactions, the greater your reach, so always reply to everyone who comments.

The next step is to use the CLAM methodology we covered earlier. (If you've forgotten, here's a quick reminder: Comment – Like – Add – Message.) And the trigger should be as soon as new prospects start to vote.

It might appear challenging to complete '**C**' (after all, you can't comment on a single vote), but you can, of course, now comment on the fact that someone has interacted. You've commented on the post, which is generally enough to justify moving to '**L**', which follows the same approach (again, you can't 'like' a vote). If someone has left a comment, you can comment back and hit 'like', but, failing that, you can always just 'like' the post in general and then move on to the all-important third and fourth stages.

'**A**': All this engagement unfolding before your eyes is the perfect opportunity to grow your audience – you need to connect/ friend anyone new who is in your target audience. You will soon notice that the percentage who accept this method is far higher than you could achieve through cold outreach – because they've already warmed themselves up for you by voting and initiating the interaction. However, never connection-request with every vote – stick to those in your target market. Otherwise, it will waste your time and confuse the members of your sales team to whom you outsource your social profile.

'**M**': This is the final stage and makes all your previous effort worth it. You've earned the right to message those who have voted, and, using our pre-set template for speed, you can whizz through and invite them all to your Weekly Moment™ event.

The example below is from one of my Monday engagement creators, taken from the LinkedIn Lead-Generation week of our 13-week cycle, which illustrates the CLAM process.

Engagement Creator: Example

Post text: I'm fascinated to see if people focus on LinkedIn as their primary platform. If yes, why? And if not, which do you prefer?

Hashtags use: #linkedinmarketing #socialmedia #linkedinleadgeneration

Question: Do you see LinkedIn as your primary social media platform each year?

Yes:

No:

(Share why in the comments.)

My first comment: LinkedIn is a powerhouse for me in lead generation, but I also love Facebook, and I find YouTube a lot of fun creatively. It's a difficult choice – I'm intrigued to know everyone else's thoughts.

My reply to voters: Hi [first name], thank you for your vote on my poll about whether LinkedIn's the primary social platform. What do you think of the results so far? I'm interested because we should focus on just one platform and go deep, not wide. Regarding LinkedIn, there are some excellent tactics to generate reach, engagement, and leads – without spending any money on ads! I'm covering these at our free event this Wednesday if you'd like to come along? You can check it out here: [link to event page]

> **Now it's your turn...**
>
> Why not post a test engagement creator before you launch your weekly events to see how interactions work? Don't make it one of your 13-week themes; take a general idea – you can use one of my suggestions above – and see how it goes.

Weekly Moment™ Promo Day

If Wednesday is your Weekly Moment™, then Tuesday is the event's big promotional push. Although at first, the idea that most of the promotional activity happens just a day before may appear a little last minute, you'll quickly find that – as the event cycle is weekly – short, intense moments of activity produce the highest yield.

In addition, going 'full promo' just before each event means avoiding overlapping promotions.

And don't forget that on social media, an audience's attention span is short, meaning someone registering and attending an event within 24 hours is pretty standard.

Bearing in mind the above, here are the three places to best promote your event:

1. Your Email List

All your activity so far will have produced an ever-increasing list of prospects' details and email addresses, which is what you need to fill your events.

Thorough testing has shown that the three Weekly Moment™ invites we suggest you send each week are ideal for gaining as many attendees as possible without over-communicating and annoying your audience.

In-depth testing has also shown the optimum time to schedule the sending of your three invites is:

1. One day before (i.e. precisely 24 hours before your start time)

2. One hour before

3. 15 minutes before

One day before: This should be a medium-length thought-leadership message that outlines what attendees need to register for your event.

Below is the one we use on the first week of our 13-week cycle, which is LinkedIn Lead-Generation week:

Title: Getting more leads

Body:

Hi [first name],

Recently, I ran a poll to over 2,000 members of our Million Dollar Sprint™ community asking, "Where is your current focus?" The winner – with nearly double the number of votes – was "Getting more leads".

So, tomorrow we'll double down on LinkedIn Lead-Generation and deep dive into this powerful platform and its ability to generate fast and targeted leads daily.

WARNING: I'll be demonstrating in a live recording EXACTLY what I do every day to generate leads organically from LinkedIn – so, as always, come ready for actionable ideas and strategy!

It'll be an interactive session with a step-by-step 'how to' swipe file for all attendees.

BUT – spaces are limited, so grab your seat at tomorrow's Marketing Round Table for a 9 am start and a 9:45 am finish.

See you in the morning.

CLICK HERE TO REGISTER

Richard, Founder, Million Dollar Sprint^{TM}

Drilling Down

Note how I start by using social proof to outline the pain – 'lead generation' – that many business owners suffer to catch readers' eyes and encourage them to keep reading, which leads them to the solution I am offering, i.e. LinkedIn.

I then turn up the heat on the value attendees will receive by using the phrases: *'demonstrating live EXACTLY what I do'*, *'actionable ideas and strategy'*, and *'step-by-step "how to" swipe file'*.

Finally, I close them into attendees by introducing the idea of scarcity and urgency with the terms *'spaces are limited'* and *'grab your seat'*.

The goal is to grab attention and create quick action. Never jump into how to solve 'their' pain at this point; simply signpost *how* they can get the 'how', i.e. by attending the event.

So keep your communication short and punchy with a clear Call to Action.

NB: We'll cover the two emails sent on the event day when we discuss Wednesday's activity.

2. Social Media

Now you have spiked the algorithm with your Monday engagement creator, the next step is to promote your event by utilising the extra reach you've created.

You can do this in two stages. The first is easy; you must copy the text from your invite email after minor tweaks, such as removing your signature and adding it to the post.

The second is to create an image for the post. Although, if you're short on time in your first cycle, you can get away without one or use something straightforward. For example, if you were promoting LinkedIn lead generation, you might use a LinkedIn logo.

However, as I mentioned in the section on branding, asking your designer to create a set of social media posts for your 13-week cycle at the start of the process is the most effective route.

To do this, create a brief that lists the 13 weeks and the time and day of each event but not the date (that way, you can reuse it each cycle). You can then use the image and your email text to create your post, which you'll send out the day before your event.

The result? A set of sign-ups harvested organically from social media.

Here is an example of one of my posts, again for LinkedIn Lead-Generation week:

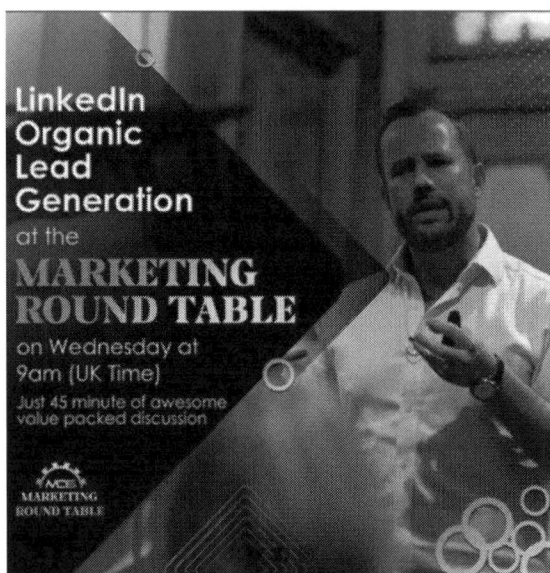

3. Direct Messages

The third place to promote your event is through direct messages (DMs).

Make sure you allocate time for this every Tuesday. In fact, I highly recommend you dedicate one hour per day – your Million Dollar Hour – to your social media rhythm.

After your first 13-week cycle, you will already have created your email and social media posts, so sending/ uploading them should take no longer than ten minutes – which leaves you with 50 minutes to hit those DMs hard!

Start by continuing to work on the previous day's engagement creator and using our template to send invite messages to those who have interacted with it. Keep an eye out for replies, as they are your cue to convince prospects to register so that they'll at least receive the replay link and swipe files.

Next, check out anyone who has interacted with your other posts or replied to your social media outreach activity. These are the perfect conversations to loop back to (especially if they've gone cold or stagnated) and invite those involved along to the event.

Remember, the more people you invite, the more likely they will attend. So use those 50 minutes to invite everyone you can.

'Share a Win' & 'What's on Next Week'

We have already covered Wednesday and Thursday, which takes us to Friday, a tale of two halves.

First Half: Share a Win

Use Friday (or whichever day is two days after your event) to increase your positioning with your audience because it is usually the first day after you've sent out the replay link as part of your follow-up. Hence, it is the day you should expect to receive some strategy session sign-ups – which makes it the perfect time to throw in a little extra credibility to help convince anyone who is wavering, that spending more time with you is a great idea.

The best way to generate credibility posts is through client wins. Don't forget; you're only ever as good as your clients' success, so always ask them to share results and successes with you in your private client group.

That way, you can take a screenshot of it and ask for their permission to share it. Once they've agreed, all you need to do is add it to a social media post.

I like to use something super simple that displays my brand and the words 'Sprinter Success'. And to accompany your post, write a synopsis of how you helped your client get their result, highlighting the main elements that relate to your flagship product to further strengthen the positioning of your service as the solution. Then finish with a strong Call to Action for your audience to book a strategy session.

Share a Win: Example

Today we want to celebrate Million Dollar Sprinter Sharon Gaskin, who launched her flagship product and sold 17 places in one hit – that's £17k in the bank. Congratulations to her – amazing progress.

If you want to discuss how to get similar results, send me a DM, and I'll set up a strategy session for us.

However, if you're launching a new product, you can get testimonials in other ways. Ask LinkedIn connections to write a recommendation for you, for example, or reach out to old clients. Even if they haven't bought your current flagship, the great experience they had working with you provides credibility.

I also suggest that, once you have delivered your first Weekly Moment™, you ask the audience for a review. Even if they haven't worked with you directly as a client yet, share that they enjoyed your training – it all helps to generate credibility.

Remember, you only need 13 to start with to tie into the weekly cycle – you can swap some of the earlier ones out once you receive more relevant and higher-quality testimonials.

> **TIP:** Add these posts to a 'Reviews' page on your website to create an ever-increasing roll call of credibility. (You can check out how we've done exactly that here: https://www.milliondollarsprint. com/reviews)

Second Half: What's on Next Week

The concept behind your 'what's on next week's post is simple, and is all about presenting the following week's theme via your Weekly Moment™ event page and gaining some early registrations.

The best time to send it is around lunchtime, as you will have already sent your 'share a win' post in the morning.

Don't forget; you've just spent an entire week discussing one theme, which means this represents a nice switch to a new concept – so pitch it hard and push it wide.

LinkedIn and Facebook have made massive improvements to their event features over the years, which means you can now invite up to 1,000 contacts per week to your event through LinkedIn, and up to 500 through Facebook – so you do need to make sure you utilise this power. In fact, these ratios may improve even further, so always keep an eye out for the latest updates.

Before you can produce your post, you need to set up an event page to follow up on all the engagements you will create with your engagement creator the following Monday. Otherwise, where would you send prospects once you start to DM them?

To realise the full potential of your event page, make sure you cover the following five elements, explained below:

1. Event banner
2. Venue link
3. Clear communication
4. Fresh content
5. Announcement post

1. Event Banner

Whether prospects are clicking on your event page or simply glimpsing it on their timeline, your banner is their first point of contact, so make sure it is professional, attractive and on point.

Also, *always* double-check you've included all the essential information. Trust me, forgetting something vital is easier than you think.

The most engaging social media posts are invariably visual, so make good use of graphics and other visual content. Again, for speed and your budget, you can ask your designer to create all your event banners in one go.

2. Venue Link

As most Weekly Moments™ are virtual, double-check that you've linked to your online venue correctly. This is one of the reasons I recommend using a Zoom registration page. That way, prospects can sign up on Zoom via your Facebook / LinkedIn event page. An added benefit is that Zoom allows them to sign up for your entire weekly series in one go rather than just the event you are currently promoting.

3. Clear Communication

An on-point event description is essential. People don't have time to read a huge chunk of text, so always share the relevant information clearly and quickly. You can use your email invites 1 and 2 as the basis, but don't just chuck the whole text in – keep your content concise.

Also, add relevant links to drive traffic and make it easy for people to find out more. Link to your speaker's bio, for example, or to previous event recordings, articles and blogs, to give potential attendees an idea of what to expect.

4. Fresh Content

Once people have RSVP'd or signed up via your Zoom link, never assume it is 'job done'. Posting fresh content to your event page helps to keep people interested, build expectations and create a buzz around your event.

The content of your 13-week cycle should already be driving engagement, but keep the conversation going by adding a post or two on your event page to say how much you are looking forward to it or to announce what the agenda will be in the chat. If your customers are anything like me, once they've registered, they'll promptly forget about it until an hour or so before, so keep prodding them.

'The higher the engagement and dwell time, the further the reach' is just as true of event pages as any other post, so make the most of any time you can spare.

5. Announcement Post

Once you have primed your event page by carrying out the above steps, it is then time to let the world know with your 'what's on next week' post.

Remember, it needs to introduce your event and explain what is in it for your followers, so make sure you include who it is aimed at, why they should attend, the pain points you'll solve, and the free value they'll gain.

This post is an excellent way to kick-start promotion, ready for your following week's daily rhythm drive, and should drive connections to your event page to find out more.

Here is a great example:

Demi van Vendeloo · 2nd
🪙 We teach you how to make money on LinkedIn and show you the bes...
1w · 🌐

🪙FREE WEBINAR: how to promote your LinkedIn event up to 1000+ attendees

What You'll Learn:
☞ 1on1 examples we used from our content plan (posts, video, polls)
☑ How to automatically invite your network throughout the month
🍮 7 'Untapped Promotion' strategies to get over 1000+ people to register for your event
🏆 How to interact with all attendees before the event and after the event

#thelinkedinoutreachacademy #linkedinevents #growthmarketing #growthstrategy #linkedintips

Once you have sent your post – remember, lunchtime is best – be vigilant for questions and registrations; otherwise, you are done with your promotion until Monday!

Lifestyle/Personality Posts

After a full-on week of Weekly Moment™-focused content, it is time to refresh your feed so the promotion for one event doesn't simply roll into another.

This is where weekends come in handy – you show your side *and* draw a line under the previous week, leaving you ready to launch a new subject on Monday.

The most effective way of doing this is by sharing fun lifestyle posts or pictures of food, events and sports. In other words, by letting your hair down a little.

Not only will this keep engagement high – which will roll straight into your big engagement creator on Monday – it will also spike conversations ready for when you meet audiences at your Weekly Moment™.

Remember, 'people buy people', so give prospects an insight into your personality. And, if you have a team, suggest they follow the same route, too.

Go Viral with Engagement Pods

Engagement pods are a great place to start if you want your 13-week cycle to go viral.

Unfortunately, they have a bad reputation as many people are confused about their purpose.

In brief, engagement pods aim to build hype around a post *before* it is popular.

They're managed via a private group (usually WhatsApp or similar) of content creators who like and share each other's posts. The theory is once this private group has created a high level of engagement, everyone else who sees the post will be more likely to read, watch, like and join the conversation.

The algorithms that monitor the popularity of each post will then show it to more of your audience, and you will achieve a snowball effect of ever-higher engagement and reach.

Spiking the algorithm as soon as you publish a post gives it the highest chance of going viral particularly if you increase engagement within the first 60 minutes. The best way to do so is by consistently creating unique content that attracts a large, loyal audience who are relevant, engaged and who comment on your posts regularly.

However, what happens if you have excellent content but because you're still building your audience, perhaps your posts don't seem to gain traction?

This situation is when engagement pods come into their own. You simply join or set one up using a WhatsApp, Messenger or Facebook group. Your fellow Million Dollar Sprinters are a great place to start, and then all agree to like and comment on each other's posts.

You can even set up automated pods with tools like Lempod or Linkboost, sit back and watch your content's reach increase as they manufacture a spike in interactions for you. Simply:

1. Install your engagement pod of choice

2. Join engagement pods related to your niche

3. Share your content, customise your audience, and gain instant reactions

> **TIP 1:** Engagement pods are an excellent way to promote LinkedIn polls as you'll gain a more extensive reach, but the responses you receive will still be actual votes.

> **TIP 2:** Use engagement pods for a few select posts to benefit from the snowball effect. In my experience, Mondays (engagement creators), Thursdays ('who wants the replay?'), and Fridays ('what's on next week') is when they're most effective.

Step 5
Create a high-converting sales process that relies on scripts and templates – not sales talent

S tep 4 – i.e. running your Weekly Moment™ and cultivating your community of perfect clients – is a beautifully rhythmic and repeatable process.

Each day, you keep to a clear and well-trodden path, knowing precisely what you should post and where you are testing and measuring for engagement as you go.

Your sales process should be no different.

Just as you did during the awareness and consideration stages, start by ensuring you add a ton of value to prospects.

As an expert, you are not an *order-taker* but an *advice-giver*, and you must keep conversations aligned with this principle.

However, as a hot commodity with increasingly valuable time, you must also unpeel yourself from sales.

The reward will be an entirely delegated sales function and a beast that needs feeding with leads for your business to scale quickly.

Unpeeling yourself from Sales

The most effective way to unpeel yourself from sales is by adding a discovery call before strategy sessions.

This 15-minute phone call uses qualifying questions to ensure each prospect is genuinely a potential client and, therefore, worth spending the time on them.

If they are, progress them to a strategy session.

Then, after the strategy session, you either close on the call or – if the prospect needs thinking time –progress them to a final decision call (again just 15 minutes) where any final questions can be asked and – ultimately – a 'yes' given.

It is a beautifully crafted system that is resolutely 'non-pushy'.

In addition, many of its elements – bookings, reminders, pre-meeting warm-up material – can be automated.

And most importantly, as both the system and all its calls are based on templates, as you scale and expand your sales team, any of its members can run with it.

In my experience, the most successful experts spend 50% of their coaching time with sales teams, helping them close deals rather than all the deals themselves.

Picture a team of commission-only, or majority-commission-based salespeople all chomping at the bit for new leads – and the sales they make are of your flagship product!

If you want to achieve this – and honestly, who doesn't? – first, you will need to establish effective training with clear parameters (in other words, a repeatable and scalable system) on how to sell using your template. That way, taking on and training new salespeople will be a doddle.

Once you have a repeatable sales process (Step 5) and salesperson onboarding system (Step 7), plus a ton of leads (Steps 2, 3 & 6), the sky truly is the limit.

So start by building your sales templates, then use them to book meetings and win clients before your new sales team even arrives.

That way, you will have the time to perfect the process and ensure all your systems work well together before you recruit your new team to run with them.

Discovery Calls

Discovery calls are a 10-15-minute phone conversation that allows you to understand more about a prospect's pain and future business objectives.

Most importantly, they help both of you quickly work out whether you are a good fit worth exploring – if not, neither of you need to waste an hour on a strategy session that never had a chance of closing a prospect into a client.

They are also the first thing you can outsource to team members, which saves you time and means you only ever pitch to qualified prospects.

The aim is to go deep quickly while building rapport using one-way questions.

Never talk about solutions or your product/service as you will be doing this in the strategy session. Simply ask where they are now, where they want to be in the future, and what is standing in their way.

Their answers will soon tell you whether they're a good prospect, and these big-picture questions will allow you to start opening their minds, making them keener to book a more extended session with you.

A bonus is that discovery calls work equally well, whether scheduled, pre-booked calls or more spontaneous and proactive. Success is more likely when you are proactive with prospects, for example, phoning someone after they've submitted an info-swap, attended a Weekly Moment™, downloaded a value bundle or completed a 5-day challenge.

As each call should be a maximum of 15 minutes, I recommend sticking to phone calls rather than Zoom sessions and starting the call with the following:

> *"Thank you for making time for my call. We have ten minutes booked to be laser-targeted, and I promise to stick to the timings as I have another call in 15 minutes!"*

Mentioning another call at the very beginning also allows you to return to it if the prospect has started to tell you their life story and the session looks overrunning. Although the best way to avoid this – remember, you need to get through all your questions in 15 minutes – is by framing questions so that your prospect's mind is working on two answers at once. For example:

> *"Tell me a bit about your businesses – who do you help? What problems do you solve?"*

Another hurdle you may sometimes face is if a prospect doesn't want to book a strategy session before they know more about the price and the product you are selling. The best way to overcome this is by saying:

> *"We don't know enough about your unique situation to be able to discuss the price and the appropriate solution yet. Our strategy sessions give you some amazing value and then, if it's*

appropriate, to look at how we can help you and the investment involved – I hope that's OK."

And remember, the above is particularly important if a team member is booking appointments for you – you don't want them giving the game away before you have had a chance to show value to a prospective client.

In the case of pro-active calls (outbound calls), don't be stumped if a prospect hasn't started – or even received – a value bundle, say. You can still push forward to see whether they qualify. For example:

"Oh, haven't you received the download yet? OK, even better – it makes great follow-on reading from this call. So I tell you what, I'll personally email it to you when we finish."

The skill lies in moving seamlessly into the qualifying questions, then – once you're sure the prospect's qualified and you know how receptive they are – to invite them to either your Weekly Moment™ in the case of colder leads or a strategy session in the case of hotter leads.

The Discovery-Call Script

The script below is for a team member making the call; if you are making the call, remember to give it a slight change in the call wrap-up sections.

Opening:

"Hi [first name], it's [your name] here from [your company]. I just wanted to see how you're getting on with [name of info-swap], plus I have a couple of further thoughts for you. Do you have a quick moment?"

If they say NO, it's not a convenient time:

"Absolutely no problem; perhaps I can call back Wednesday morning or Thursday afternoon?"

If they say YES:

Q1. *"Great, did you receive the [info-swap name] and what were your initial thoughts?"*

Q2. *"... and why were you interested in the [info-swap name], and where did it catch your eye?"*

Q3. *"Tell me a bit about your businesses – who do you help? What problems do you solve?"*

Q4. *"... and if you had a magic wand, where would you be 12 months from now – the top three things, say?"*

Q5. *"What's stopped you from reaching this 12-month target so far?"*

Q6. *"Is fixing this [or these things] something you want to get sorted sooner or later?"*

"Thank you for sharing with me – I have a page full of notes, but I guess the main points are:

Recap 1

Recap 2

Recap 3."

If they are a hot lead:

"From what you've just shared, I'd love you to spend some time with our founder Richard Woods in a strategy session to look at where you are now and to suggest strategies for you to reach your targets for the future.

In the session, he'll share screens and draw models for you to apply to your business.

From brand awareness and lead generation to flagship-product creation and customer advocate programs, it's a full-on 45 minutes of value.

If that works, I have his diary open so I can book that call with you now ... Great!"

Then book them straight in (ideally within the next day or two).

"Thank you again for the call, and I look forward to checking back in to see how you found the session with Richard."

After the call, don't forget to send – or make sure one of your team does, using your second 'personal' email account as discussed in Step 4 – a personal thank-you. You should include a booking confirmation and a pre-strategy session preparation video or guide in addition to your booking software's auto-generated email confirmation. And, whatever else you have promised, such as the info-swap.

If they are a cold lead:

"We host a complimentary group Zoom at 9 am every Wednesday, which we call our Marketing Round Table. It's just 45 minutes of Facebook ad demos, funnel creation, landing page critiques, LinkedIn growth hacking, email marketing sequence ... and many other marketing and sales subjects.

It's free to join, and I'd love to book you in if that works for you?

Great!"

Then book them straight in via the Weekly Moment™ Zoom registration link.

"Thank you again for making time for my call, and I look forward to checking back in to see how you found the Round Table."

Just as with hot leads, don't forget to email a personal thank-you that includes their booking confirmation, the info swap and/or any other resources you promised to send on top of Zoom's auto-generated booking confirmation.

TAKEAWAY: The simple scripts and process I have outlined above will allow you to bring in team members who can use them to follow up on the leads you create and squeeze as much opportunity from your marketing as possible.

Strategy Sessions

Strategy sessions are the primary sales moment of your funnel.

All roads end here, so it's time to blow your prospects' mind with the value you add before you close them on your flagship product.

You aim to make the time you spend with each prospect feel consultative, which means you want them to do a lot of the talking – so make sure you ask plenty of burning questions and give them space to open up.

You will be asking them to invest a significant amount at the end of the session, so you need to take them on a journey. One that moves them from a position of possible scepticism, to the realisation that they need your flagship product/service to fix their pains.

Luckily, to make things easier, the structure and script that follow have been thoroughly battle-tested by me, my team, and your fellow Sprinters. And all of us use them to close big deals every day.

But don't forget; the below is a guide, not a fixed script. Write out your version, learn it, and then remember to be flexible. Neither you nor your prospects are a robot, so don't treat strategy sessions as if you were.

1: Build Rapport and Connection

"Hi [first name], this is [your name]. How are you today?

I'm calling for your [branded strategy session name]. Are you ready to get started?"

Small talk:

- Draw on connections, bridges, and heartstrings

- Build rapport (you're making a friend)

- If they're a referral, ask them how they know [insert name of the person who referred them].

Set up the call:

"So, if you're ready, shall I set up the call and then we can dive in?

We'll have about an hour together, and I'll be asking questions to learn more about you and your goals – but rest assured, everything you share will remain completely confidential. Together, we'll:

- *Look at what you want your world to be like in 12 months*

- *Paint a picture of where you are now*

- *Then I will present what campaign/process will help get you to the 12-month target*

- *Finally, we will explore if there's a natural fit for us to work together.*

I hope that's all OK and meets your expectations for this call?"

2: Explore What They Want

"So [first name], when it comes to [insert topic], if you had a magic wand, where would it be 12 months from now?"

Once they've replied, mirror back to them what they've said by listing the key points. Ideally, focus on the area(s) where your flagship can help, then use your following sentence to make their 12-month goals more personal:

"What will that mean for you on a wider scale?"

Continue to use similar questions to drill down into their deeper wants, needs and desires until you get an emotional response. You will know when you have got there when they start to use terms such as 'freedom', 'confidence', 'to get out of debt', 'to travel', 'to increase my savings', 'to make a difference'.

Curiosity is your best tactic, but be genuine and always come from the heart: this is where people can get emotional, so they need to feel safe opening up to you.

3: Explore Where They Are Now

"OK, great. So if that's where you want to be 12 months from now, where are you now? In other words, where are we starting from?"

Be curious and use active listening to help them list their answer exactly.

4: Establish the Gap

Next, establish and explore the gap between where they want to be and where they are now by digging into their pain:

"What's stopping you – or has stopped you in the past – from achieving that?"

Keep digging to make this pain a 'here and now' thing:

> *"What's not doing this costing you?"*

> *"What will happen if you don't get a handle on this?"*

Make sure you are really present with them until they genuinely feel the pain of not achieving their 12-month target.

5: Paint a Picture

> *"I'm now going to paint you a picture of everything I've heard, felt, and seen so far."*

Use this time to recap the main points they've made. Let them add to your list, making sure you note down any additions.

The skill lies in listing their points in a way that will support your ultimate pitch.

6: Build Credibility

> *"Before I jump into some ideas, what inspired you to reach out now?"*

Remember, use active listening to mirror their answers back to them.

> *"Why me? How did you find me?"*

If they saw you speak, watched a video, or listened to one of your podcasts:

> *"What did you enjoy about it the most?"*

> *"Would it be OK if I shared a little more about myself, so you have a sense of my background?"*

Then, mention your top-three credibility highlights – but make sure they're relevant, and you list them in a way that relates to your prospect's specific situation. For example, I might say:

"I started my business as a freelance graphic designer and grew the company to 28 staff and one million in revenue."

Now it's your turn...

List your three credibility highlights below:

1: _____

2: _____

3: _____

7: Introduce your Strategy

"Now let's look at how we can solve this for you and get you your 12-month wand-wave target."

By giving them a solution, you earn their trust by showing your expertise and giving them actionable ideas to achieve their 12-month target.

- Don't rush things, but don't go on too long either – ten minutes is usually the sweet spot.

- Drop in references to your solution(s) throughout – but don't dive into pitching (that comes later).

- Reference stories and/or client results that support your ideas as this will help seed your service for later.

"How does that sound? Any thoughts?"

Encourage them to share their thoughts and answer their questions until they say the magic words: *"How can you help?"*

This response is the cue you've been waiting for to switch into your pitch.

However, if they don't say it, here is a backup plan to get them to sit back and start listening instead of talking:

> *"My intuition's telling me that we could help you. Are you interested in learning more about how we could be a good fit to work together?"*

8: Move into your Pitch

> *"OK, great. Well, this is how it works …"*

Replay where they are now in your process/methodology/service. Draw it out for them as you explain, or show them your Journey Map or a graphic of your methodology for even more impact.

Walk them through each stage of your service and how you can help them achieve their 12-month goal(s) more quickly, easily or cheaply. Then let them recap their thoughts by asking:

> *"What do you like so far?"*

Next, condense your 'how it works' demo into a quick recap of the benefits they'll achieve:

> *"So, as a recap, here's what you'll get …"*

For example, for the Million Dollar Sprint™, I might say:

> *"A daily drop-in clinic means we can review your progress, answer any questions and share screens if you're stuck. It's also a great way for you to maintain – and gain – momentum."*

Now it's your turn...

List your program benefits below (more or less than six is fine, too):

1: _____

2: _____

3: _____

4: _____

5: _____

6: _____

9: Share Success Stories

"Let me share a few success stories from other businesses I've worked with like yours ..."

Share a couple of client success stories and relate them to your prospect's specific situation and goals. If you don't have any paying clients yet, share your own stories, or describe how you've helped people more informally. The important thing here is the transformation you helped them make – i.e. the before and after – and how this relates to your prospect.

Customise how you frame each testimonial to make it super relevant.

Now it's your turn...

List the names of three clients you've helped to succeed and include a brief note on why each is such a great testimonial to use. Adding photos of clients and/or screenshots of their testimonials into your presentation will bring this to life:

1: _____

2: _____

3: _____

10: Detail your Offer – and Move on to the Price

"So, I hope you agree you're a great fit for [name of your flagship product]."

"Now, apart from price, do you have any other questions?"

Answer their questions until they reach the point at which they are only interested in cost, then say:

"You could easily pay $20,000 for a similar solution ... and that doesn't even include [list the elements of your flagship that your competition doesn't provide] – which I still believe is well worth it if you get the result of [their magic wand target].

... but, bearing in mind we wanted to make our program affordable and accessible to people who need it, the regular investment for [your solution name] is just $10,000."

Make sure you let that land with a pause.

Add a time-scale bonus:

"I also have some good news. We reward decisive action – after all, being decisive is the same energy you need to be successful in your business – so if you say 'yes' today [or end of the week, month, etc.], you'll save an additional $4,000 with our decisive action bonus. You'll receive the entire [flagship name] for just $6,000."

If you have a payment plan, offer the option here.

11: Close the Deal

"Are you ready to get started? Is that an option for you?"

If 'yes':

"OK, great! I'm ready for your credit card whenever you are."

It will now be appropriate for your target market to process their credit card there and then on a virtual terminal or, if you don't have one, on your website's buying option or Stripe Checkout (a prebuilt, hosted payment page).

If you have to send a proposal or an invoice (typical when selling to corporate), then make sure you take control of the follow-up and book a decision call (more on this later in the chapter). It should be a few days after the strategy session to ensure they do not let the all-important 'getting started' drift and get forgotten about.

Make sure you let them know what happens next, too. For example:

"Look out for our welcome email, which contains all the info about what's in your program. I'll also send your schedule, dates, and logistics confirmation."

Please include any other next steps they need to know about, but keep it simple and don't overwhelm them with too much detail. They've made a big decision, so you must keep their excitement high.

If 'no':

> *"OK. What else do you need to be able to make a decision?"*

Go back to exploring the gap and flirt with their objections. If this doesn't work, you could offer a no-fail guarantee:

> *"Assuming you've fully worked the program, if you don't see results within _____ days/months, I'll work with you until you do."*

Offer 90 days or even up to a year. I recommend extending their program with your group component until they see the results you've promised.

Another option is to throw in a 1:1 coaching session. Trust your intuition on the fastest way to get results for them.

Another objection you are likely to come across at some point is:

> *"I'm sorry, but I can't afford it now."*

In which case, you should reply:

> *"OK, can I ask you a question about that? If it wasn't for the money, is this something you'd want to do?"*

Then go deeper by asking:

> *"What would you need to get out of the program to make it worth your time, money and effort?"*

Once they've answered, reassure them that is precisely what they will get, then go on to say:

> *"So, if money's still the issue, would it be helpful to brainstorm some ways of how you could generate it?"*

If it is just the money, start to think laterally by working out payment plans, money-back guarantees or offering them the first month free.

Once you've got them to say 'yes', process their credit card as above and start your onboarding.

Decision Calls

Sometimes your client may need time to think. If so, the best way to handle it is by offering a decision call, when you can bring the whole process to a head to get that all-important 'yes'.

Usually, decision calls will be a 15-minute Zoom to handle any final questions and then move them into onboarding.

You can follow our example email below to confirm a call. However, to prevent things from drifting, always make sure you book a time and date for one – ideally within two to three days – before you end the strategy session.

If anyone says 'no' to a decision call, understand why before you try to change their mind. For example, if it is simply a 'not now' then agree on a date to check back in with them in a couple of months.

Decision Call: Email Example

Email Title: Thank you for the call

Email Body:

Hi [first name],

Thank you for the call. I'm delighted that you're considering [name of your flagship].

Attached is our Information Pack, which goes to prospective clients – it's a great starting point as you consider joining us.

Just as a quick recap, here are the T&Cs: [insert]

The cost for [name of your flagship] is $_____

After the 90 days, you'll keep full access to all live sessions, group calls, VIP groups and online course content, including new events released through the year at $_____ per month.

That's it! I look forward to checking in with you at 11:30 am on Tuesday via the following Zoom link: https://zoom. us/j/6391733884

Kind regards,

[your signature]

Handling No-Shows

In any business, when you're setting up meetings, whether it's a first-time sales presentation or trying to move a sale forward with a decision call, there'll be people who don't show up. Trust me, I've been there!

To a great extent, of course, the rate depends on your type of business, the processes you have in place, and your relationship with clients.

Using our sales-focused system, you'll often properly meet prospective clients for the first time during a discovery call or strategy session. They may already have come to one or two of your Weekly Moments™, but only as part of a larger audience in which it is almost impossible to form an individual connection with them.

This situation means that your no-show rate might be higher than you would normally expect – but don't panic. The good news is that as long as you follow up promptly, many of your no-shows will show up to their next meeting.

So, how do you follow up most successfully?

The No-Show Sequence

Creating a process that allows you to follow up on missed appointments easily is critical to getting that next meeting. After all, the Million Dollar Sprint™ system depends on prospects attending strategy sessions to move sales forward.

So, if a prospect misses a meeting, your goal is first to understand why, then to re-schedule as soon as possible so you can turn them into customers.

Start by refusing to get frustrated – remember, these things happen to the best of us and trying to guilt-trip someone will only create friction. They already know you're busy and that they've wasted your time, so reminding them of this will only kill the credit you are holding in your back pocket and make them less likely to meet with you in the future.

Instead, take a concerted approach to find out why they missed the meeting. Something big – or bad – may have come up.

Keep exchanges professional, and only use channels you have previously used to communicate. Your goal is to be persistent without making them feel pestered.

Once you've established the reason for a missed appointment, continue to help no-shows consider you – even within the conversion stage of your sales process – through additional education. After all, including added value at the rebooking stage is a classy way to continue to build an appetite for what you do.

So conclude your communication with helpful information such as links, swipe files, Weekly Moment™ replays, and podcasts to really up the value of your follow-up.

That way, no-shows will quickly realise they need to be part of what you provide.

No-Show Follow-Up: Email & SMS Templates

Initial Email

Email Title: [first name], let's try this again

Email Body:

Hi [first name],

It looks like we couldn't connect as planned today. I appreciate that things come up that take priority. However, I remain confident you'll find a highly productive conversation about [name of your flagship product /service].

Shall we set up a time to reconnect? Here's a link to my calendar: [insert link].

In the meantime, I thought you'd be interested in a recent video we created that will help you [insert video benefits and link].

All the very best

[email signature]

You can even add more links in a P.S. – you aim to ensure the prospect continues to consider you.

Initial Text Message (SMS)

Hi [first name], sorry not to see you today. I appreciate things come up. Let's rebook our chat about [name of your flagship product /service]. Here's my calendar: [link].

In the meantime, check out our free training on [video name and link].

Thanks again, [your name]

Second Email: The Nudge

Sending a second email shows you're serious about seeing someone and value the session.

Keep it short and snappy, but, as discussed in Step 4, include your initial email so that your prospect has all the information they need in one place. If you're sending emails manually, reply to your first email to do this. Or, if your email is part of an automated sequence, you can achieve the same effect by copying and pasting your first email below your new one.

Tip: Automated emails ensure communications remain bespoke by removing the date and adding names as a dynamic field in the email 1 section.

Email Title: Bubbling this back to the top of your inbox

Email Body:

Hi [first name], following my email a few days ago, I just wanted to bubble this back to the top of your inbox as I'm keen to work through a few strategies with you to help [you/your business] achieve [insert result].

Let's get a rescheduled date in our diaries – here's a link to my calendar: [link].

Thanks again

[email signature]

Second Text Message (SMS)

You can also throw one final text into the mix, letting them know that it is your last message – say one day after your initial one:

It's my last attempt to align our diaries, [first name]. The strategy session I'm trying to rebook is full of value, but if it's not to be, then I understand and will pull back. My calendar's here if you're in: [link].

TAKEAWAY: Carrying out the process will allow you to use the experience you gain to perfect both it and your scripts. However, once you close deals and find your diary crammed with appointments, it's time to move on to Step 7 to build a team who can take it over.

In the meantime, in Step 6, we'll look at how paid ads and automation can help you build a higher volume of leads, placing further pressure on your diary and eventually enabling the smooth creation of a sales team.

Step 6
Crank up the volume of leads through paid ads & automated outreach

By Step 6, you will have a system that generates opportunities through organic outreach and a process for warming your audience through daily content and your Weekly Moment™.

You've also created templated sales scripts and automation that allow you to perfect and delegate every stage of your sales process.

That means it is time to flood your funnel with leads. After all, all you and your sales team need to succeed, is an abundance of opportunity!

Step 6, as the following diagram illustrates, is about speeding up the factors at the top.

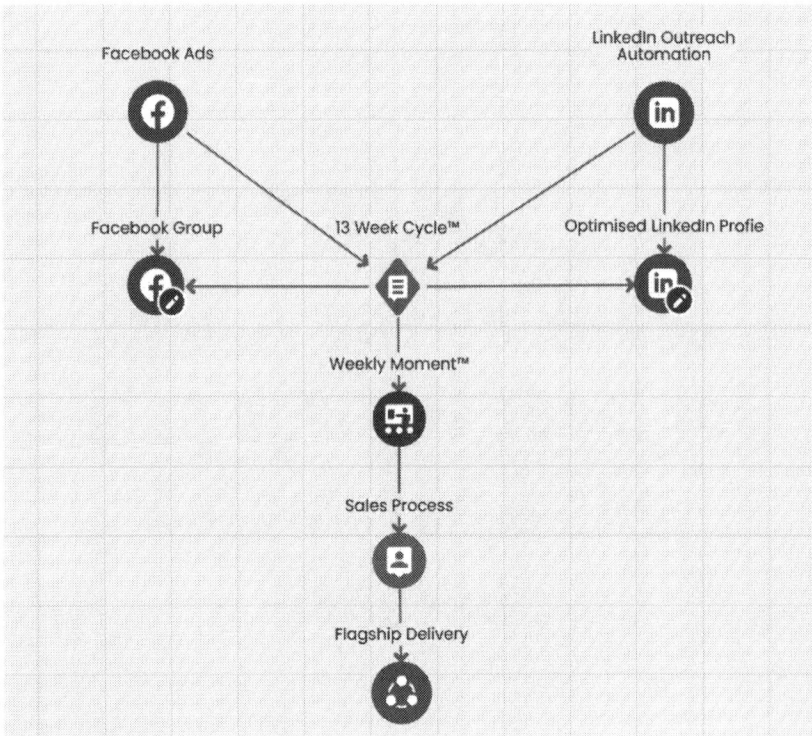

Facebook Ads

LinkedIn Outreach Automation

Facebook Group

13 Week Cycle™

Optimised LinkedIn Profie

Weekly Moment™

Sales Process

Flagship Delivery

Paid Ads

What better way to create an abundance of opportunity than to unleash the power of paid ads?

Many businesses make the mistake of thinking they can start here rather than working through all the steps we have just taken together first. As a result, you'll often hear them claiming: *"Ads just don't work for me,"* or *"They're too expensive."*

This type of response illustrates a lack of understanding of the value of a lead and the importance of a warming-up funnel. A flawed process and/or team to work on every single prospect means losing out on a mountain of opportunity.

But luckily – and thanks to our Million Dollar system – that's not you. So now you have your Weekly Moment™ and your sales system in place, it is time to dive in.

Paid ads are one of the quickest ways to help potential customers discover your brand and what you offer. Rather than waiting for them to find you organically, you take a shortcut by purchasing advertising that allows you to specifically target your audience.

Although paid ads aren't limited to one platform, if you're already using Facebook, I recommend you keep things simple by sticking to Facebook Ads. That way, you can go deep on this one platform rather than spreading yourself too thin.

To create a Facebook ad, define your target customer, using criteria such as location, interests, demographics, previous purchases, and other pages visited. You can upload a list of prospects or customers – set a maximum budget, say $500, and then let the ad run until your budget is used up.

Your goal is to create a focused campaign that pushes audiences down your sales funnel and into booking a Weekly Moment™ or strategy session – although in the latter case, don't forget to set up a discovery call first to filter out any unqualified prospects.

An added bonus is that by tagging each prospect as a lead from ads, you'll also be able to measure ROI.

I have found a great tactic to create a targeted video sales letter (VSL) with a booking link for a strategy session. Using these micro-webinars as the destination for ads helps you quickly generate trust among your audience, and you'll find you get many strategy sessions booked straight off the back of them.

On the following page is an example of a VSL training session on the Million Dollar Hour we send paid ads to. The 'Let me show you how' button goes straight to a strategy-session booking form.

Another bonus with paid ads is that you're not limited to an A/B testing methodology. Instead, you're free to test any variables until you spot a trend and style that work so you can keep moving in that direction.

One simple test is to keep the ad's copy the same but to try different images. If it turns out that pictures of you work best, you can try out other photos of you – always aiming to drilling down deeper and refine your creative style.

For example, ads such as the following to promote our Marketing Round Table all feature different images of me, as we have found they work better than other graphical variations.

Multiple tests of a similar themed ads set iterating around one successful ad always trying to improve upon the cost per lead

Once you've discovered which ads work best, crank up the volume so your funnel fills with opportunities – ones that go on to convert into calls at an acceptable cost per strategy session. Don't forget, your newly created scripts mean the close rate of your strategy sessions will start to stack up, too.

The more you spend, the faster you'll grow.

Automated Outreach

According to a study in 2019, 75% of marketers were already using automation, and the number was continuing to grow – which means marketing automation is here to stay.

The beauty of automation is that it allows you to do things quickly, affordably, and accurately, so when it comes to LinkedIn, make sure you harness its power for lead generation.

The other good news is that LinkedIn's automated outreach system works in a similar way to that for paid ads. In other words, you use tools to show your message to more people within your target audience.

On LinkedIn, for example, you can use tools to create automatic connection requests and DMs that don't require you to create these yourself.

You can use the same systems described in the LinkedIn section of Step 2. However, adding automation to pre-load a connections campaign with potential opportunities means you can sit back and let the software work through the list by sending connection requests and pre-set messages.

Although many tools can conduct automated outreach for you, I believe that in choosing Expandi, we have partnered with the safest and most effective. (As a bonus, they've kindly given us a discount code for Sprinters –email the MDS team if interested.)

TAKEAWAY: Make sure you harness the power of paid ads and automated-outreach tools to increase the daily volume of leads you produce from your chosen social media platform(s).

After all, you need to feed your funnel – and it's hungry!

Step 7
Recruit a commission-based sales team

When most business owners think about sales teams, they usually do so too late. Not only should you set up a sales team at the same time (or very soon after) you start Step 6, but you also need to consider them skill-set specific and make sure they're dedicated to just one part of your funnel.

The mistake many people make is to employ someone for sales who manages the business's social media and telephone outreach – all while being expected to close deals.

In reality, finding someone with this set of hybrid skills is impossible. And, even if you do, they'll still tend to be better at one – which means sales opportunities are likely to be lost.

The solution is to recruit specific, part-time, third-party contractors who can focus solely on one of these skills.

That way, you can recruit for each speciality and tailor your training, tracking and resources to their skill set when the new team member joins, so each of them is in the best position to succeed.

It is the most agile and cost-effective way to approach your sales-team budget and is by far the most efficient use of your time, as you can make sure each element is working flawlessly before you move on to the next.

Generally, I suggest recruiting for two skills to start with:

1. Prospector – responsible for finding and qualifying leads into strategy sessions.

2. Closer – responsible for handling strategy sessions and converting leads into clients.

Once both work well, you can officially remove yourself from sales and leave your team to succeed. You have to turn up your system's ads and automation dials to grow your lead volume, your team, and the sales that go with them.

But, to dig a little deeper into these vital roles first, a typical job description for a **prospector** would be:

- Handling inbound enquiries from marketing campaigns and authenticating/correcting any data. If you've run lead-generation campaigns before, you will appreciate this. For example, many people don't use capitals at the start of their name or submit forms under the name 'hello kittycat!', so having a pair of eyes to check and edit each lead before it joins your database is pure gold.

- Managing organic outreach to online communities and progressing potential sales opportunities. For example, a prospector would handle organic outreach such as 'Trojan Horse' posts in Facebook groups or engagement creators within your 13-week cycle.

- Building rapport and developing relationships with each potential client once the lead is generated, by continuing the conversation via DMs until a discovery call is made.

- Managing manual or automated LinkedIn outreach to potential leads who may start as cold and require warming up via a sequence of DMs.

- Making discovery calls to qualify each potential opportunity and then book them into a strategy session – where your closer(s) take over.

- Producing handover documents for closers outlining why a lead has been qualified and progressed into a strategy session.

- Adding all notes produced to your CRM and updating the RTM dashboard with lead volumes, discovery calls and strategy sessions booked.

Once you've employed this person, you'll find you are excellently placed to increase your volume of strategy sessions – and that this increase in the number of pitches you're able to conduct will very soon be mirrored by the rise in sales.

If you're still responsible for pitching, the second person in your team becomes key.

A typical job description for a **closer**, then, would be:

- Confirming each strategy-session booking with a 'looking forward to meeting you' email, introducing you and your business further and supplying any pre-meeting resources necessary.

- Conducting each strategy session to close the deal during the call.

- Conducting decision calls if one is needed.

- Managing all follow-up and next-stage processes for both 'yes' and 'no's.

- Taking payments for sales, then moving each new client to the start of the onboarding process and handing them over to your delivery team.

- Updating your CRM with notes and the RTM dashboard with show-up rates and sales-close figures.

Once you have people with these two skill sets, you can sit back and watch your business grow.

Recruiting your Sales Team

As we discussed in Step 1, I start with the return-to-work market whenever I need to build skill-specific teams.

For example, as my lead-generation agency was based just outside London, I found many people who, generally for family reasons, didn't want to return to commuting into town every day. Although we might not have been able to pay the most, we could offer the flexibility they wanted and, as a result, triumphed with highly skilled applicants.

A great place to tap into this market is via a simple post to your local Facebook groups – we used 'The Windlesham Community' or 'Camberley gossip girls & guys'. Here is an example post:

> *"Hi all, I'm looking for part-time help with my business. It would be 3 hrs a day, 4 days a week and mainly involve phone calls to confirm people attending a weekly event. It's home-based and nice and flexible – but the experience is important. Let me know if you can help/know anyone who's looking. Thanks all."*

After filtering through all the applicants, we were able to recruit a great team who went on to become our prospectors and closers.

Managing your Sales Team

Employment is an inherent issue for many service-sector businesses – usually due to difficult conversations around holding staff accountable to targets, keeping them focused and giving clear directions on our expectations.

Owners often find managing everything difficult; initially, discussing these elements is easy. Training is delivered in a focused way once a team member is embedded into the project, as the owner tends to move on to the next project. However, this is when things can slip.

To get around this, I advise not managing your team directly but using an RTM (Reporting, Targets & Management) dashboard to do it for you.

A robust RTM dashboard (a templated version is available through our online portal) lets prospectors and closers know precisely what is expected of them and how they can succeed in their roles.

A section of our templated Sales RTM Dashboard

MY WEEKLY STATISTICS:								
WEEK	TOTAL LEADS	LEADS TARGET	DISCOVERY CALLS	DISCOVERY TARGET	STRATEGY SESSIONS	STRATEGY TARGET	SALES CLOSED	SALES TARGET
4 Jan 2021	89	60	3	3	7	3	4	1
11 Jan 2021	63	60	3	3	3	3	3	1
18 Jan 2021	76	60	6	6	2	3	2	1
25 Jan 2021	68	60	20	9	5	3	1	1

The example above sets a weekly target for each key deliverable. By filling it in, each salesperson can then compare where they are against their target.

In other words, the dashboard essentially manages each team member for you.

Your role is to concentrate on coaching team members to help them reach or – even better –smash their targets. If you spot their numbers dipping, for example, you loop back to help them improve on the areas they find most challenging.

As a tool, it is simple but hyper-effective – particularly if you allow people to see each other's targets. There's nothing like a little healthy competition to drive leads and sales!

Step 8
Implement a profit system to accumulate founder wealth alongside company growth

While at first it is natural to focus on consistent business growth, never forget to mirror this with a sustained increase in personal wealth. I have seen too many entrepreneurs increase turnover exponentially and yet, at the end of the month, not have enough cash to pay their bills – let alone buy a decent holiday or a Lamborghini!

In theory, it's simple: subtract costs from sales and whatever is left is yours to take as profit – and even to blow at the weekend if you wish!

In practice, however, we entrepreneurs are emotional beasts with a weakness for the new and shiny, which means if we are not careful, we can soon empty our bank accounts each month buying things we think our business needs. And the last thing we remember – by which point it's often too late – is to pay ourselves.

I first ran into this issue myself with my lead-generation agency. Whenever we won a new project, I would hire someone new to handle it. In fact, I became a real collector of people, hiring as many new employees as possible.

Although our turnover was huge, at the end of the month, there was rarely any cash left to pay me. The money went on rent for the office space, salaries – even lunches out for everyone which tended to turn into big expensive parties!

Something had to change.

Inspired by Mike Michalowicz's excellent book, *Profit First*, I switched to a pay-yourself-first system.

In his book, Michalowicz applies Parkinson's theory – *"mass expands to the room you give it"* – to bank accounts, whereby people's spending expands to match how much they have in their accounts.

To combat this, he suggests picturing your spending as small plates at a buffet, making you eat less as you can't fit as much on them.

What this means for your business is that instead of having just one plate, you have six (in the form of six different bank accounts), each of which you allocate a percentage of your income. Then, once or twice a week, you divvy up the payments received in your income account to transfer them to a different account, each representing a specific budget ring-fenced for essential expenditure.

It is the most effective method I have come across to protect yourself from raiding money that should go to the tax office, for example – and from spending your profits, too.

Below are some example accounts and percentages based on what I – and most of our clients – use. Incidentally, as a bonus, the figures helped me realise my operational expenses were too high and I needed to make cuts.

1. **Income Account:** 120% of income from sales (i.e. amount invoiced plus VAT) is paid here, ready to be distributed to your other accounts.

2. **VAT Account**: I strongly recommend using this to handle your VAT payments – immediately adding your 20% VAT to it leaves you free to reallocate the net 100% left in your income account. Be aware that as you can reclaim VAT, the account will run at an excess. (As Michalowicz's book focuses on the USA system in which a VAT account isn't needed, I've adapted this for UK and EU clients – adjust percentages to relate to your location.)

3. **Profit Account**: Here is where you allocate a percentage of your income as profit. As your income is handled elsewhere, it is a *retained profit* account for use as your rainy-day fund or any significant capital expenditure. For this reason, keep the percentage light at 5%.

4. **Owner's Comp**: This is your income account to lock in your take-home salary. I suggest allocating 50% of net income to it – knowing you're getting half of whatever your business brings in is a nice reward!

5. **Tax Account**: You need to allocate 15% of net income to this for corporation tax. Many countries have a 19% or 20% rate, but remember: rates are calculated on profit, whereas you're saving 15% of net *turnover*, which means this account will always show a healthy excess.

6. **OPEX Account**: This is for operating expenses, including spending on your team, ads, software – and anything else you need to run your business. Limiting the amount you allocate to this to 30% of net income makes you shrewder with your cash and focuses your mind on the most important things.

Remember, you can use the excess from your VAT and tax accounts to help pay your income tax bill – so essentially, the 50% in your owner's comp account is an after-tax figure.

All this is exciting news when you consider that scaling to a million in revenue will net you $500,000 in personal income *after* tax!

You can take this model further by using it for your wealth. For example, I have adopted a similar multi-bank-account approach to transfer money into different personal pots, including 'Investments', 'Disposable', 'Bills', 'Holidays', 'Cars' and 'Schools'.

Knowing that every $1 your business brings in represents income that will trickle down to all parts of your life is fun and even a little mind-blowing.

It is also why having a wealth strategy set up before you scale makes sense. After all, **understanding the cash-allocation system outlined above will make the goal of scaling your business more personal and its success vital.**

8 Steps: Conclusion

Embarking on any business-growth journey can initially seem overwhelming, so having a system as your guide and a process to start building your campaigns is invaluable.

Remember, you have the support of me and my team every step of the way. Whenever you're stuck or unclear on something, simply reach out and we'll be there.

To sign off – and to make sure you're super-primed for success – here are a few of the keynote pieces of advice we commonly give to clients:

1. **Rome wasn't built in a day**: Make sure you approach each of the steps with a T-NAD mindset, i.e. try it (T) first; then, once you've got it working well, you'll have nailed it (N); at which point it is time to remove as many of the human elements as you can through automation (A); then finally to recruit a team member to whom you can delegate (D) it.

2. **As you grow, stay flexible**: Whenever a business makes a false start – or needs a complete overhaul – I always follow my gut instinct to make the necessary changes. Our client can then drop the new system back into their business and – boom! – they have momentum and structure.

3. **Leaky funnels are normal**: You may find that although you're growing a big following on LinkedIn, for example, not

enough of them are booking onto your Weekly Moment™. Don't get disheartened – you may need to work on your event titles or how your invitations are distributed. Your goal isn't to avoid leaks but to trace and patch them as you go.

4. **Never become a bottleneck**: Once leads start coming in and those who've attended an event need follow-up, and your diary is filled with appointments for strategy sessions, you should be delighted – and rightly so. However, remember that you will cause a bottleneck if you are still responsible for duties. In order to avoid missing important opportunities, once your systems are working, build a team to keep pace with them.

5. **Start with awareness**: You can't do anything without an audience, so always start by building your database and a social following. Together, they produce the prospects you'll market to and in turn, invite to your Weekly Moment™.

6. **Have fun and experiment**: Our system is particularly great because it offers you a robust and structured process. Remember to let your hair down a little and reveal your personality with eye-catching titles and fun posts. People buy from people – so give them plenty of 'you' and never be afraid to experiment.

So – that's it!

I hope I have helped to persuade you that using our system will raise your profile and flood your business with leads.

It's one hell of a journey – and I'm excited to join you!

Richard

Next Steps

We've introduced our Million Dollar Sprint™ system; the next step is to show you how to apply it to your specific business. To do so, why don't we spend 45 minutes together to discuss your growth goals and look at how a scalable lead-generation system will help you achieve them?

We'll answer questions such as:

What your perfect Weekly Moment™ should be

How to build that vital sales machine into your business

When is the best time to build a team

What your flagship product is and how to make it truly scalable.

It is an action-packed session that entrepreneurs who attend can't believe we don't charge for – with one calling it: "The most valuable session I've had all year."

So don't delay; reserve your seat today by heading to the link below right now: https://www.milliondollarsprint.com/MDS-Strategy-Session-Application

Acknowledgements

Special thanks go to Debra Levitt and her team. Without their support, I would not be able to focus and access the creativity required to write books, build courses, and coach clients.

This book also would not have come together without the excellent help from my book editor Harriet Powney. Working through her funny, upbeat, and fabulous comments are a joy. If she were marking my homework, her red pen would have run out of ink! It was a mountain to climb to get these chapters into shape, and I thank her for doing so effortlessly.

I want to thank Brenda Dempsey of Book Brilliance Publishing and her team for swiftly polishing and agreeing to publish this book and making it available from the world book trade, not just Amazon.

I also want to thank the Million Dollar Sprint Mentors who help me to support and coach our Sprinters – Anthony Stears, Jake Liddel, Susan Payton and Nathan Littleton.

Penultimately, I want to thank the Million Dollar Sprinters themselves. Your growth is the reason why I do this. Keep pushing because your success keeps pushing me to be the best I can be for you – thank you.

Finally, I want to thank my family – Mum and Dad who raised me to be creative, entrepreneurial, and free-thinking. Cara, who is my world, keeps me on my toes but stops my head from hitting the ceiling. Finally, Poppy and Mylo, ultimately, it is all for you xxx

Further Reading

Books by Richard

Brexitpreneurship: How to win from Brexit (independently published, 2017)

Digital Trailblazer: Harness Technology and Marketing to Rapidly Grow Your Business (ReThink Press, 2015)

Other Further Reading

Ferriss, Timothy, *The 4-Hour Work Week: Escape the 9-5, Live Anywhere and Join the New Rich* (Vermilion, 2011)

Hormozi, Alex, *$100M Offers: How To Make Offers So Good People Feel Stupid Saying No* (Acquisition.com Publishing, 2021)

Keller, Gary, *The One Thing: The Surprisingly Simple Truth Behind Extraordinary Results* (John Murray Learning, 2014)

Michalowicz, Mike, *Profit First: Transform Your Business From a Cash-Eating Monster to a Money-Making Machine* (Portfolio, 2017)

Michalowicz, Mike, *Clockwork: Design Your Business to Run Itself* (Portfolio, 2022)

Priestley, Daniel, *Key Person of Influence* (ReThink Press, 2014)

About the Author

Richard Woods is a bestselling author, award-winning entrepreneur, finalist of the top BBC series *The Apprentice*, keynote speaker, radio presenter and investor.

He runs the Million Dollar Sprint™, which works with entrepreneurs to scale their service businesses to a million in revenue and beyond.

Richard's first book, *Digital Trailblazer*, went straight to being the #1 Best-Seller on Amazon and continues to sell globally. His second book, *Brexitpreneurship: How to Win from Brexit*, also went straight to #1.

In 2015 he was a finalist on the BBC series *The Apprentice*. During that time, he was the top seller across all tasks (winning eight out of ten, which is second on the all-time list) and broke two records: most sales in one day (£4.3 million); and "The best advertising task ever seen on *The Apprentice* – credited by Lord Sugar himself.

Awards he has won to date include Young Entrepreneur of the Year (Haines Watts), Key Person of Influence (Dent Global), and Marketing Campaign of the Year (Inspire Business Awards).

Richard also makes regular appearances on Eagle Radio, BBC Surrey, BBC Sussex, Marlow FM and Brooklands Radio. He is a frequent speaker at sizeable business events, trade shows and seminars.

He studied Business with Entrepreneurship at Southampton Solent University, receiving First-Class Honours for his final dissertation, 'Is there a link between Dyslexia and Entrepreneurship?'. He was later awarded an honorary MBA for his contribution to business.

Notes

Notes

Notes